FINDING THE BLUE SKY

FINDING THE BLUE SKY

A Mindful Approach to Choosing Happiness
Here and Now

Joseph Emet

A TarcherPerigee Book

tarcherperigee

An imprint of Penguin Random House LLC
375 Hudson Street
New York, New York 10014

Most TarcherPerigee books are available at special quantity discounts for bulk purchase for sales promotions, premiums, fund-raising, and educational needs. Special books or book excerpts also can be created to fit specific needs. For details, write: SpecialMarkets@penguinrandomhouse.com.

Library of Congress Cataloging-in-Publication Data
Names: Emet, Joseph, author.
Title: Finding the blue sky : a mindful approach to choosing happiness here
and now / Joseph Emet.
Description: New York, New York : TarcherPerigee, an imprint of Penguin
Random House, LLC, [2016] | Includes bibliographical references.
Identifiers: LCCN 2016022074 (print) | LCCN 2016031868 (ebook) | ISBN
9780143109631 (paperback) | ISBN 9781101992364 (ebook)
Subjects: LCSH: Spiritual life—Buddhism. | Happiness—Religious
aspects—Buddhism.
Classification: LCC BQ5670 .E44 2016 (print) | LCC BQ5670 (ebook) | DDC
294.3/444—dc23

Printed in the United States of America
1 3 5 7 9 10 8 6 4 2

Book design by Elke Sigal

Contents

CONTENTS

The deepest desire in each of us is the desire to be happy and to bring happiness to the people and living beings around us.

—THICH NHAT HANH,
  Under the Rose Apple Tree

All men seek happiness.* This is without exception. Whatever different means they employ, they all tend to this end. The cause of some going to war, and of others avoiding it, is the same desire in both, attended with different views. The will never takes the least step but to this object. This is the motive of every action of every man, even of those who hang themselves.

—BLAISE PASCAL,
  Pensées

---

*Please excuse the androcentric wording. Pascal, who lived in the seventeenth century, was following the conventions of his time.

Notes to the Reader

We are what we think.
All that we are arises with our thoughts.
With our thoughts we make the world.
Speak or act with an impure mind and trouble will follow you
As the wheel follows the ox that draws the cart.
Speak or act with a pure mind
And happiness will follow you as your shadow, unshakable.
—BUDDHA, *The Dhammapada*

With these verses, Buddha hands us the keys to his kingdom, for today's thoughts will form tomorrow's habits, and tomorrow's habits will form our character, and our character will affect the course of our lives. Pretty soon, you are talking about destiny—something people have imagined as being written in the stars.

But do this in reverse, and you are back where you started from—to thoughts. And thoughts **can** be changed—it often happens spontaneously, but we can also do it intentionally with mindfulness. Now, work forward, and you are soon changing destiny without having to travel to the stars.

Picture a dog following its nose. During the days when we had a dog, we found it rolling in a pile of manure more than once. It had found the manure by following its nose as we let it run loose in open fields.

Now picture a hummingbird. Unlike a dog, it has almost no

sense of smell. It follows its sense of sight. For a hummingbird, brighter is better, so it ends up in brightly colored flowers sipping sweet nectar. It spends its days enjoying flowers.

The hummingbird and the dog are programmed by nature, but unlike these two animals, we have the ability to change our programming. We can, if we have vision and persistence, learn to change our ingrained patterns of thinking, and train ourselves to be more like a hummingbird. We can form beneficial new habits. William James, the pioneer of American psychology, considered habit so important that he wrote a treatise on it. This is how it begins:

"When we look at living creatures from an outward point of view, one of the first things that strike us is that they are bundles of habits."

He continues, "Any sequence of mental action which has been frequently repeated tends to perpetuate itself; so that we find ourselves automatically prompted to think, feel, or do what we have been before accustomed to think, feel, or do, under like circumstances, without any consciously formed purpose, or anticipation of results."

William James had no illusions about the strength of habit and conditioning. He observed that habit "alone prevents the hardest and most repulsive walks of life from being deserted by those brought up to tread therein . . . It holds the miner in his darkness, and nails the countryman to his log cabin and his lonely farm through all the months of snow."

We may continue with, "And it keeps the grouchy grumpy, the pessimist gloomy, the lonely alone, the anxious worried, the stressed tense, the depressed sad, the aggressive combative, and the angry mad."

But there is hope for change.

James considered that we can learn to "make our nervous system our ally instead of our enemy. For this we must make automatic and habitual, as early as possible, as many useful actions as we can, and guard against the growing into ways that are likely to be disadvantageous to us, as we should guard against the plague."

Each of these "ways that are likely to be disadvantageous" is the focus of a chapter in this book. In addition, each chapter contains exercises for developing specific habits that will move us toward happiness. Those exercises are found in the Time for Practice section of each chapter. It takes practice to change habits, for our habits live in the unconscious. If we are to succeed in changing them, we must reprogram the unconscious. Use habit formation to your advantage. Dancers do it, musicians do it, athletes do it, and all those who learned a new language have done it. As I was learning the T'ai Chi form, I was conscious that I was learning a new set of habits—a new way to move, where movement is initiated from the center—and giving up old habits such as my round-shouldered posture. Habits are not all negative; beneficial new habits can be learned.

Think of each chapter of this book as describing another condition for the flower of happiness to grow in your life.

After you go through the book once, you can open a page at random, and see what that section has in store for you today. Or you can glance through the Table of Contents and pick a practice that seems appropriate for the day. You can download it at Mindfulness MeditationCentre.org/finding-the-blue-sky/ and work with it. The practice supplements are an integral part of this book. You will find that they will grow on you as you use them.

Introduction

Introductory Story

. . . .

Don't Forget to Be Happy!

As he was taking his leave of the Zen master, the young student put his hands together and bowed.

"Don't forget to be happy," said the master.

The student appreciated this parting gesture from his teacher. "Thank you very much. Although I have not been here long, I appreciated my stay, even though I didn't always do everything right . . ."

The master interrupted him: "I'm not wishing you a good trip. I'm teaching you."

"Oh . . . ," said the student.

Note: Each chapter of this book has three sections: a story, a text designed to stimulate reflection, and a practice section with exercises. The text that follows the story is not necessarily an interpretation of it. The three sections each throw light on the subject of the chapter from different angles.

1

Time for Reflection

. . . .

I believe that happiness can be achieved
through training the mind.
—THE DALAI LAMA

Of the two well-known Buddhist teachers of our time, Thich Nhat Hanh smiles and the Dalai Lama laughs. In the Dalai Lama's case, a cheerful temperament and a happy upbringing have converged to make him "a professional laugher" as he self-describes. In his book *My Spiritual Journey*, he elaborates: "My cheerfulness also comes from my family. I come from a small village, not a big city, and our way of life is more jovial. We are always amusing ourselves, teasing each other, joking. It's our habit."

Thich Nhat Hanh, on the other hand, is "a professional smiler." He says, "If we are peaceful, if we are happy, we can smile and blossom like a flower, and everyone in our family, our entire society, will benefit from our peace." His saying, "Sometimes your joy is the source of your smile, but sometimes your smile can be the source of your joy," is also true of laughter—body and mind are one. Wherever one goes, it pulls the other along. It does not matter which one takes the first step.

"Those who understand jokes are many; those who understand true laughter are few," remarked the eighteenth-century Zen master Hakuin Ekaku. Do we only laugh because something is "ha-ha" funny? If so, we may have to wait a long time between laughs! Like a smile, laughter expresses a sense of cheerfulness and joy. Being alive is sufficient reason for feeling both. Cultivate those states of mind, and stay in touch with them all day long.

Wisdom, good humor, and lightness of spirit go together with these Buddhist masters—they are inseparable. A sense of humor is a basic survival skill. You may say, "But life is not always a bowl of cherries." Thich Nhat Hanh will agree with you. But he will add, "You need to smile to your sorrow, because you are more than your sorrow." Which is it for you—that the sun occasionally shines through the clouds, or that the clouds occasionally obscure the sun?

As you do the practices in this book, your outlook will gradually lean more toward the latter description, for the sky is actually more than the clouds. And your mindspace will gradually include more of the energy of mindfulness and a deep sense of humor about things. It will be more spacious.

Each day of our life contains more poetry than all the poetry books in the world. Our heart is full of longings, our mind full of wishes. Our life is the most precious thing in the world. We not only want to protect it; we also want it to flourish, to thrive.

Mindfulness can help us realize that wish. It can help us change in beneficial ways, for mindfulness is the peculiar ability to observe oneself objectively—this is a necessary prelude to change. Mindfulness is that quality of awareness and self-observation that is missing in robots. That lack severely limits the usefulness of robots, and makes robot-like people dangerous to themselves and to others.

❁

I am the custodian of "this," and not so much the owner. As a custodian, I'm still discovering better ways to take care of its physical and mental needs, still wondering if I ate too much for supper last night. I'm still learning how to guide its emotional life, like a captain guides a boat on the open sea. The sea can sometimes be wonderfully calm—an image of serenity, with the golden sun, playful waves, and a refreshing breeze. It doesn't require much effort or skill to guide the boat of the self at those times. We may get the feeling that mindfulness is not necessary. The captain may go to sleep—and wake up with a jolt when the drifting boat hits a rock. Think of a time when a challenge seemed to come out of the blue and shook you deeply.

At other times, the sea can be agitated—the waves higher, the winds stronger, and the temperature colder. Then, more skill is needed from the captain. There are many chilling environments, such as cruel dictatorships, that we humans have created here on Earth. Did we create these because we did not regulate our own emotional thermostat well? There are places, whole countries, that are in turmoil, like the sea in its wild moments. Did we create these conditions because we did not know how to deal with our own inner torments? "Peace in oneself, Peace in the world," wrote Thich Nhat Hanh. This is the direction peace travels—from the inside toward the outside. Despite what many people think, this also turns out to be true of happiness: "True happiness must come from inside." These words from the beginning of Thich Nhat Hanh's book *Anger* leave me with disturbing questions: Did we create all the misery, injustice, and wars in the world because of our own unhappiness? Because we did not know how to find happiness inside?

❧

Some people are born into wealthy families. Others become wealthy by dint of hard work—because they want to. These two paths also intertwine in determining our happiness level. And since we cannot choose our parents or our genes, I will be focusing on mindfulness practices, because if you weren't born happy or into a happy family, you can still increase your happiness level through them.

Many people view happiness as something that just happens. They are not aware of the myriad choices that happy people make as they go about their day, sometimes unconsciously—routines that are the mental equivalents of brushing teeth. Yes, there is a genetic factor to having a sunny disposition, just like there is also a genetic factor to having good teeth. But that is not all there is to it, just like the genetic factor is not the only cause of good teeth.

❧

Would you just walk out into the traffic on a busy highway?

Do you take regular showers, and use deodorant?

Do you nourish your body with regular meals?

We care for our body in these and many other ways as a matter of course.

Our mind also needs care and attention—it also needs to be regularly cared for and nourished. There are also accidents and collisions waiting to happen in the depths of our heart if we do not take care to avoid them with mindfulness and kindness. If we do not look after our mind in the same regular way that we care for our body, we can suffer as a result.

The Buddha said, in effect, "I have taught one thing and one thing only, how we make ourselves unhappy, and how we can stop doing that." When we are unhappy, we are wont to blame outside circumstances for causing our unhappiness. Here, Buddha is pointing the finger at self-inflicted unhappiness—on our inner life, our attitude, our habits, and our explanatory style. Join me in exploring these, for when the dark clouds are blown away, the blue sky is instantly there—we do not have to go looking for it. Follow me, chapter by chapter, as I set out all the ways we can use mindfulness to increase our happiness level.

The practice sections are the heart of this book—they are the agents of change toward a happier outlook. There are two exercises per chapter, twenty-four altogether. I personally know well all the pitfalls I describe in the twelve chapters of this book. I fell into them and climbed out of them many times before I learned to stay out of them. Do the exercises more than once. They are the ladders out of the pitfalls of unskillful habits. Even better, they are the bridges across those pitfalls. Make this book your companion for a month. Let it guide and inspire your meditation practice as you read it.

Chapter 1

Regulate Your Moods

Time for a Story

. . . .

Blown Away by a Puff of Wind

A celebrated poet of ancient China went to see a Zen master who was an old acquaintance. The master was out. The poet decided to wait, and was ushered into his study. Seeing a notepad on the desk, he started writing verses. At the bottom, he signed, "The devout Buddhist who cannot be moved by the power of the Eight Worldly Winds." In that tradition these are gain and loss, sadness and joy, praise and ridicule, insults and compliments. After a while, seeing that the master was still not back, the poet left to go home.

When the master returned and saw the poems, he added at the bottom, "What garbage! Even a fart is better than these!" and sent it back to the poet.

The poet was furious. He rushed back to the master and vented his rage: "I thought you knew me better than that! What gives you the right to put me down in such a crass manner? You know that I'm a devout Buddhist."

"Hmm," said the master with a smile, "the great Buddhist claims that all the winds of the Earth cannot move him, yet he is now blown all the way here by a single puff of wind from the bowels!"

Time for Reflection

· ·

Think of the mountains, rivers, and the great Earth
as your meditation pillow,
and of the universe as your personal meditation hall.
—HAKUIN EKAKU

We are always balancing our bodies so that we do not fall and hurt ourselves. We do it unconsciously and routinely, but that does not mean that it is easy—we have conveniently forgotten how long it took us to learn to walk as a toddler. We do not remember what a thrill it was when we no longer needed training wheels on the bicycle. We overlook how walking is a challenge for many elderly people, some of whom can no longer regulate their own balance, and must depend on walkers or wheelchairs. Many of the people who are wearing a cast on a leg or an arm have momentarily failed to regulate their balance. The result has been painful. The consequences of losing emotional balance can also be painful.

Balance Is Dynamic
In his statues the Buddha looks as if he is always perfectly balanced. Some people take this as a model to emulate. But this is the wrong model—because we are alive and unlike a statue, we are often out of balance; physically, as we get hungry, thirsty, or sleepy, and emotionally, as we do our relationship dances or our work pirouettes.

Balance is another word for peace.

A statue is always in perfect equilibrium, but it does not go anywhere or do anything—it does not move. Our proper goal is to be aware of it when we get pulled or pushed off-balance so that we can right ourselves and not fall down. Walking or running involves a playful attitude to balance, and a certain amount of confidence. Similarly, the balance of a bike rider is not static; it is dynamic. The reason the biker does not fall down is not because she is never out of balance. The reason is that she is aware of slight variations in equilibrium, and compensates by steering—she steers herself toward balance.

Life is like riding a bike.

In a statue of the Buddha we do not see the *process* of balancing; we only see the *result*. We do not see the tugs and shoves of feeling and emotion. If we imitate his statue we may only succeed in becoming emotionally dead. When we imitate the process of balancing, on the other hand, we encounter the art of mood regulation, or mood maintenance.

The Dance of Happiness

Like a bicycle rider, happy people may look as if they are never out of balance—but this is an illusion, and the rider is in fact responding skillfully to slight changes in equilibrium. Put a statue on a bike and give it a push. You will see what happens. The statue crashes because it is not aware of the first sign of a change in balance. It does nothing to maintain its equilibrium. A happy person is not like a *statue* of the Buddha; she is more like the *real* Buddha—she is more like a bike rider. She is aware of pressures on her state of mind, and practices mood maintenance just like a biker constantly practices balance maintenance.

Emotional balance needs to be achieved dynamically, because we are pushed and pulled in all directions by our children, relationship partners, parents, and bosses. Happy people maintain a positive mood the way a biker maintains balance. They are mindful of the pressures on their mental state, and respond by self-regulating. In contrast, unhappy people are easily thrown off-balance, because they are not tuned in to themselves—they do not know it when they begin to lose balance. Their focus is usually outward. They are focused on what others are doing "wrong," and they keep losing their own balance more and more until they fall.

Those who are happy are adept at recognizing internal and external pressures. They feel the pull-and-push, and maybe experience a slight leaning before it becomes a serious loss of balance—they are good at mood maintenance. They come back to vertical instead of continuing to lean till they fall. This skill has become second nature to them, perhaps because they learned it as small children, or because they were born with a more acute sense of mindfulness. Some happy people will explain their mood maintenance skills if you question them—they know what they are doing. Others do it unconsciously, but equally well. In the Buddhist tradition, mindfulness is not considered to be a mental state we have to learn from scratch. We all have it to some degree, but in some of us it may be buried deep in our psyche. Like kindness or contentment, mindfulness can be close to the surface, or it may lie deeper down, but its seeds are there in all of us.

I did not learn happiness skills from my parents as I grew up. My early upbringing was more like a hands-on course in unhappiness. My parents were not good practitioners of mood regulation. My dad was often off-balance, veering dangerously toward anger at the slightest bump in the road, and my mom toward sadness. They stayed stuck in their sullen moods, and did not right themselves when they fell into them—a bit like a toddler who wails helplessly when she falls down and hurts herself. My parents gave me the gift of life, but they could not give me the gift of happiness because they did not have it themselves.

In my early years what I gleaned about happiness came from watching my best friend and his family. I was fascinated by the mix of warmth and positivity that reigned in his home, and spent as much time as I could there. It was like an adoption, except that in this case it was the other way around—I had adopted his family. The

difference in mood between the two households was remarkable—
like the difference between an abandoned field where mainly thorns
grow and a spring meadow where different kinds of attractive flowers bloom. Later on, I found myself naturally gravitating toward
other happy people, looking at them with a mixture of fondness and
wonder. Happiness remained a kind of fascinating magic for me for
many years, until I started practicing with Thich Nhat Hanh. Initially, it was his happiness that drew me to Thich Nhat Hanh—I
saw him as one of these magically happy people.

But Thich Nhat Hanh also provided me with practices for going toward happiness in my own life—he taught me mindfulness.

Mindfulness and happiness are related. Just giving advice—
such as providing lists about what to do in this or that situation—
does not often work, because it is a challenge to remember such
advice when we are stressed. When we are stressed, our field of vision narrows, and we revert to old habits. The variety of stressful situations we encounter in life is endless. Here is a short list:

A traffic jam. Not getting a coveted raise. Unexpected illness.
Not being able to find what you are looking for when you go on an
errand or shop. Getting a traffic or parking ticket. A disappearing
cat. A power failure when you are just starting to make supper. Not
being able to sleep on a given night. An extra piece of work or a request for overtime thrown your way. A cancelled appointment.
Weather forcing a change of plans. Your partner saying, "Not to-
night, dear." Kids getting a bad report card, failing, or getting into
trouble. Teenagers misbehaving. Your favorite coffee cup falling on
the floor and shattering. Getting bumped off a flight because of
overbooking. Things not going your way at work. Boyfriend or girlfriend trouble.

So many bumps in the road. If a bike rider falls down on every
bump, she will always be bloodied—and worse.

Expectations and Disappointments

Changes and disappointments are challenges to mood regulation. Taking them in stride and adapting to unforeseen circumstances easily, even gracefully, is part of the secret of happiness.

Buddha focused on the changes that are part of every life. Gorgeous hair, beautiful skin, and firm muscles are all impermanent. Parenthood—in the sense of a house full of animated children—is impermanent, as kids get older and leave. At some point, health changes turn into health challenges. Thich Nhat Hanh elegantly summarizes Buddha's teachings on impermanence and suffering by putting the accent on expectations: "It is not impermanence that makes us suffer. What makes us suffer is wanting things to be permanent when they are not." Expectations and disappointments are like night and day—they are opposites that nevertheless go together.

Disappointments affect every one of us at one time or another, regardless of our happiness or positivity level. What matters is how strongly we react, and how long we take to recover from them. It is a fact of life that we run into roadblocks of one type or another during the course of an ordinary day. Mentally go through the last few days of your life—if you are like me, you will find that each day had its share of them. How strongly we react to these determines whether we make ourselves unduly unhappy over them or not. How long our reaction lasts determines how long our unhappiness continues.

Are you able to regulate your mood and return to a baseline of pleasant functioning soon after a setback?

Buddha pointed out that change in one guise or another is the rule rather than the exception. His contemporary Heraclitus expressed that teaching in an unforgettable though androcentric metaphor: "No man ever steps in the same river twice, for it's not the same river and he's not the same man." Yet, if we look closely, we see that Buddha's teachings on impermanence are not only philosophy. They are focused on a particular purpose: reducing human suffering. Here is an example: "All conditioned things are impermanent. When one sees this with wisdom, one turns away from suffering." Buddha is emphasizing not only that change and impermanence are facts of life. He is also saying that we suffer if we do not accept that. He is showing us the way out of suffering.

However, expectations are also part of life, just as much as change. It is also important to accept that. We all have them. A dancer does not ignore or deny gravity—she dances with it. Trying to live without expectations is not the goal—expectations give meaning to life. When I eat, I expect that the food will satisfy my hunger. Otherwise I might not eat at all. I might play cards instead until I starve to death. When I get in the car, I expect that it will start. The trick is in not becoming prisoners of our expectations. It is to accept that our expectations do not *control* the world. Our expectations are part of *us*, but in the world there are many causes and conditions that determine how things will function. These causes and conditions are all subject to change as well.

Hiding

Crabs run away and hide for safety when they are afraid. Rabbits hide in their holes.

Negative energy does that to many of us as well. Some of us tend to isolate ourselves emotionally and physically when things are not going well. Be mindful of your spirit during a period of self-imposed isolation. It is rest that heals us—rest your mind by practicing serenity meditation. Make sure that your time alone is not spent in self-bashing or in mentally bashing another, but in understanding and the compassion that inevitably follows understanding. You can also listen to a practice song to guide yourself toward positivity.

Without mindfulness, we tend to overreact to disappointments instead of accepting them as part of life. "Overreactions are best understood as intense responses that are fueled by past experiences and raw emotions that have not been carefully sorted out," writes Judith P. Siegel in her book *Stop Overreacting*. This jumble weighs us down. It is more of a challenge to get out of the way of a car coming at you if you are carrying lots of baggage. You are less nimble. Mindfulness practices such as "Letting go" and "Calming the mind" help us stay light in body and mind.

What is important is that the skill of toning down our reactions to unpleasant surprises can be learned. First, decide that this is an important matter, important enough to invest the time and energy it takes to tackle the task of habit change. Happiness is made up of a constellation of traits. Mindfulness affects many of these traits in a beneficial manner, and by undertaking mindfulness training we can reduce stress and increase happiness.

Wisdom and Positivity

Shakespeare described Buddha's observation that sickness, old age, and death are part of our lives in poetic terms:

> . . . Last scene of all,
> That ends this strange eventful history,
> Is second childishness and mere oblivion,
> Sans teeth, sans eyes, sans taste, sans everything.

It has been pointed out that anxiety is a normal reaction to this state of affairs. If you knew that there was a lion around the corner waiting to devour you, would you not feel anxious? Martin Seligman associates depression with feelings of helplessness—and we are all helpless when it comes to avoiding that lion. Our helplessness increases as we get closer to the corner—up to 50 percent of the elderly living in nursing homes suffer from depression.

Anxiety and depression are closely related, and they are not conducive to happiness. Buddha pinpointed three attitudes that contribute to those mental states.

IGNORANCE

This is the kind of ignorance that is the opposite of wisdom.

In a poem, Thich Nhat Hanh invites us to visualize a forest. If

14

you look closely, you may notice that a few of the trees are sick and dying. But the forest looks fine, verdant and inspiring. When you visualize a forest, the forest is what you see and admire, not the individual drama of each particular tree. Every living being in the forest is an inseparable part of the whole: the birds that carry seeds around, the bacteria that populate the soil and help the roots assimilate nutrients, the wasps that pollinate the trees—these do not exist separately from the trees. Even the birdsongs. They all evolved together. "No tree is an island," to borrow a metaphor from John Donne.

If a tree saw itself as an island separate from the ecosystem, somehow living independently of the soil, the air, gravity, the mushrooms that recycle nutrients, and the Earth itself, it would be seriously deluded. If it saw its own life span as defining the beginning and the end of existence, it would be ignorant in the Buddhist sense.

If we view our life and life span as entities separate from the river of life, we are likewise deluded. We are ignorant of the basic facts of life, no matter how "educated" we may otherwise be.

Such an outlook makes us unhappy. Martin Seligman writes in his book *Learned Optimism* that "we belong to a society that grants to its individual members powers they have never had before, a society that takes individuals' pleasures and pains very seriously, that exalts the self and deems personal fulfillment a legitimate goal, an almost sacred right." However, absolute and lasting personal fulfillment is impossible to achieve in this world, even for absolute dictators. Seligman observes that "the age of the self is also the age of that phenomenon so closely linked to pessimism: depression, the ultimate expression of pessimism."

Ignorance does not see the Tree of Life—it only sees individual leaves; more specifically, it sees the one individual leaf that is itself. It finds life meaningless because it does not think in terms of relationships, family, community, or ecosystem. Those larger entities add meaning to our individual lives. When we identify with the tree instead of with an individual leaf, the falling of any one leaf does not feel like the huge tragedy that it otherwise appears to be. A sense of humor about death is possible. There is less likelihood of anxiety and depression.

Ignorance is a well-chosen word for this outlook, as it suggests a lack of understanding about how life works. By helping others, an individual in an ancestral community understood that she was also helping herself. There was no distinction. I shared the life of a small traditional pueblo in Guatemala some time ago. In that community, exile was the punishment for repeated criminal acts of egoism. Indeed, most crime is an expression of egoism in one form or another. The pueblo had neither the resources nor the will for building a fortified prison for criminals. If an individual acted solely out of self-interest, ignoring the interest of the community, he or she was exiled. In the past, exile often meant death, for it was difficult to survive in the wild without the support of a group. Unfortunately these days it mostly means a bus ride to the capital, Guatemala City, which partly explains the high rate of crime in that city.

Seen in the light of Buddhist wisdom, compassion is not only a "nice," virtuous feeling for others; it is the only reasonable attitude toward our fellow creatures. The wisdom of this attitude is coming home to us. As we act without regard for the well-being of other creatures, as we degrade the environment, our own happiness, or even survival, is threatened. According to a recent UN report, there are now twenty million eco-refugees worldwide.

CLINGING

William Blake wrote:

> *He who binds to himself a joy*
> *Does the winged life destroy;*
> *But he who kisses the joy as it flies*
> *Lives in eternity's sunrise.*

Clinging is the wish to make the impermanent permanent. Ultimately, our individual lives are impermanent—this realization drives the mindfulness mantra "Be Here Now." This mantra says, "Enjoy each moment of the impermanent life instead of clinging to it." The same understanding applies to lesser things. A new item of clothing brings pleasure, but that pleasure is impermanent like everything else. If we crave that pleasure and want to experience it again and again, we soon run out of closet space. What the Buddhists call "craving" leads to the "hedonic treadmill" or "hedonic adaptation" described by psychologists. It is more than craving things. It is craving the *pleasure* that having this or that will bring. There is a difference between buying an item of clothing because you need it, and buying it for the thrill. Unfortunately, the item of clothing lasts longer than the thrill it brings when it is new.

There is a similar difference between eating because you are hungry and pleasure eating. The first one nourishes you. The second one alters your pant size.

Consider that most of us have more clothes than we need, eat more than we need, and have a bigger or more powerful car than we need. Our houses are larger than what we need.

Ignorance and clinging, as well as the next topic—aversion—describe dead-ends in our quest for happiness.

AVERSION—NOT ACCEPTING WHAT IS

We usually think of forgiveness as forgiving people who have hurt us.

But it is also possible to think of forgiveness as forgiving people for being who they are.

Forgiving teenagers for being teenagers.

Forgiving fusspots for being fusspots.

Forgiving people of a different race or nationality for being different.

And for those who are sexist, forgiving women for being women, and men for being men.

Shaking crying babies until they are injured, violence against women, and racism are examples of the inability to forgive people for being who they are.

At first glance, this may appear to be different from what we usually understand by forgiveness, yet acceptance and forgiveness are first cousins.

Lack of acceptance shows itself in various ways—as ill will, annoyance, anger, irritation, or animosity. Buddha observed that some people's annoyance and anger seem to be etched in stone. For others these states of mind are like writing on water. He said, "Imagine a certain person who, even though spoken to harshly, sharply, roughly, is easily reconciled and becomes agreeable and friendly, just as writing on the water soon disappears."

Buddha was describing mood maintenance. Here he speaks of it as a character trait, but he spent most of his life teaching mindfulness practice (part of the eightfold path) so that the stone engravers can learn to write on water instead. This transformation starts with awareness of being a stonemason. It continues with awareness of the ill effects of that way of being. The next step is a deep wish to change. Finally, it is also necessary to have the good fortune to encounter mindfulness teachings—an indispensable tool for making the change.

Trade in your stone-carving tools for mindfulness.

For best results, the rest of the items in the eightfold path—such as diligence, concentration, and vision—are also required, for some people forget their deepest wishes in a blink.

Time for Practice

Using the Practice Material

There are six guided meditations and eleven practice songs at Mindful nessMeditationCentre.org/finding-the-blue-sky/.

You can either listen to them directly from the MMC website or download them to your own device first.

To practice with the guided meditations, sit in the meditation posture and follow the spoken instructions. To practice with the songs, use them to take a meditation break during the day. You can do this as you take a walk outside, or when you are in a train or a bus. Take advantage of any free time you have. The purpose of a meditation break is to bring you back to a meditative space during the course of the day. Each song only takes three or four minutes. Allow the song to become an earworm.

To practice with the meditation themes, read the instructions before you sit for meditation, and let them inspire your meditation time. Practice several times with each theme.

Guided Meditation: Practicing Mood Maintenance

Wisdom is often glimpsed first in retrospect, or by observing a quality that is missing in others. At that point, it is not yet wisdom—when we observe how quickly and for "no reason" toddlers lose emotional balance, for example, we do not automatically become wiser. We do not necessarily become wiser even when we recognize the same mechanism at work in some adults, but we are now starting to draw close. We get even closer when we recognize that when we ourselves lost balance on a past occasion, we were, in some respect, being childlike. This is "retrospective wisdom." Getting stuck there is a recipe for much regret and guilty feelings. It saps our energy, and worse, it prevents us from being in the moment. True wisdom happens here and now, in real time.

Free your mind from regrets. Take a deep breath, and stay with breath-consciousness. Then, take a minute or two to get into the meditative space, and contemplate each question or instruction below, one by one.

> *Sit with a straight back.*
> *Notice that keeping your back straight makes room for the*
> *breath in your abdomen.*
> *Breathe very slowly, filling your abdomen with each breath—*
> *six slow counts in, six counts out.*

> *What percentage of you is here now?*
> *Where is the rest of you?*
> *Why is it there?*
> *Bring more of you here by concentrating on the physical*
> *sensations of breathing.*

> *Are you looking outward now, thinking of others,*
> *or are you looking inward?*
> *Remember, other people are only triggers—*
> *they trigger our fear, insecurity, love, or anger.*
> *Those feelings themselves are inside us.*
> *Please note what feelings are being triggered now.*

Are other people or situations passing through your mind?
Also notice the feelings they trigger.
Take your time, and stay with each feeling as it comes up.

※

Now, add mindfulness to the mix.
Mindfulness is like the energy with which the mother embraces
a crying child.
Mindfulness is that kind, comforting presence inside you.

※

See each emotion as the mother sees it—with kindness,
but also with a touch of humor and lightness of heart,
with a smile.
Slowly shift from focusing on your emotions to focusing on
mindfulness,
from being the toddler to being the mother.

※

The mother is not carried away by the toddler's emotions.
She stays calm and peaceful.
That's why she can bring comfort to her child.
That calm and peaceful energy is also in each of us.
Call upon it now, and stay with it as you breathe in and out.

As you repeat this exercise, you awaken the soothing power of mindfulness. We all know this energy—we were all picked up and comforted many times by a kind mother when we were distressed as a child. In some of us, that energy may have receded through lack of repetition, or through other life circumstances, and it may have become out of reach. Repeating this exercise brings it closer to the surface. Repeating it often makes it a constant presence in our life, allowing us to build resilience and emotional balance.

Practice Song: The Sun Is Shining

> *Suppose you are morally squeaky clean,*
> *but there is no music inside. Then what?*
>
> —KABIR

Music is a huge part of our lives—it is the enchantment behind many of our ordinary activities. Notice that just about everyone walking in the street or riding the bus is wearing earbuds or earphones. Practice songs aim to harness the power of music in the service of mindfulness. This song is the first of eleven in this book. To practice with it, visualize the sun.

Now visualize it shining in your heart.

Become a source of light, burning bright.

Instead of complaining about or suffering from darkness, just illuminate it.

> *The sun is shining in my heart,*
> *As it shines above the clouds.*
> *It gives me warmth, it gives me light*
> *Through the day and in the night.*
> *Shine, shine, shine, my sun,*
> *Shine through the clouds, shine through the fog,*
> *Warm, warm, warm every heart,*
> *Wherever I go.*

When light and warmth are not coming from the outside, find them inside.

Warm up the winter.

Light up the night.

Chapter 2

Be Aware of Your Story

Time for a Story

. . . .

The Zen Master Who Talked to Himself

His students would often hear a Zen master talk to himself. The conversation usually went something like this:

"Master!"

"Yes?"

"Be awake, be alert!"

"Yes."

"From now on, don't be fooled by anyone!"

"Yes, yes!"

Time for Reflection

. . . .

Now, I have met the builder of the house and broken
the ridgepole.
I have destroyed the rafters.
That house shall not be built again.

— BUDDHA, *DHAMMAPADA* (#154)

There is the story of our life.

It may change as we grow and mature. It may also change according to who is telling it: you, your spouse, or your children. It may even change according to whom you are telling it to.

Then, there is the story of each day. This is the story you tell your partner at the end of the day when she or he asks, "How was your day?" We may assume that what we say reflects what actually went on, but be aware that there is room for much interpretation there.

There is also the story of each moment. There is a generous amount of interpretation there as well: "I carelessly broke the glass" may become "Somebody carelessly put the glass in my way."

Who are these stories about?

In a vacation rental in Mexico last year, my neighbors, two men in their late thirties, kept me up until 4:30 A.M. several nights in a row. Groggy with sleep, I was imagining them with mouths as big as a crocodile's—they were talking so loudly. At first, this seemed to be a story about "poor me" and "those drunks," but I also suspected that there was more.

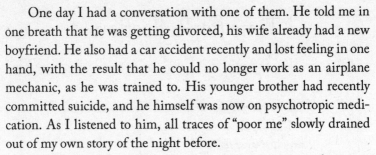

One day I had a conversation with one of them. He told me in one breath that he was getting divorced, his wife already had a new boyfriend. He also had a car accident recently and lost feeling in one hand, with the result that he could no longer work as an airplane mechanic, as he was trained to. His younger brother had recently committed suicide, and he himself was now on psychotropic medication. As I listened to him, all traces of "poor me" slowly drained out of my own story of the night before.

Seeing things from only my vantage point turns everything into a personal drama. But there was more than my personal drama here. There was also the drama of my neighbor. The unfaithful wife and the other driver on the road also have their own stories. I can only begin to see those stories if I have peace and compassion in my heart. And some space.

In an old Zen story, a person tells the teacher that he is feeling lonely and miserable, and wants to know what to do. The teacher answers, "You have drunk three glasses of the finest wine, yet you are complaining that you haven't even wet your lips."

My noisy neighbor had three beautiful children, who are those three glasses of fine wine in this story. He also had an attractive wife, and owned a comfortable house—more glasses of fine wine. His wife wasn't there to tell her side of the story, but I wondered if his car accident and impending divorce had something to do with his propensity to drink too much and stay up all night. There are stories within stories. I had a feeling that my neighbor was busy constructing a "poor me" story out of the events of his life.

Usually, we think that our story and our self are separate entities. Focused meditations such as the ones at the end of this chapter make it possible to see that the two are not so separate. "Who am I?" in one guise or another is a common meditation theme in the Buddhist tradition. Buddha attained enlightenment in part by concentrating on this question. The verse that introduces this chapter was reportedly what he said after his enlightenment. Buddha had seen that he had constructed the self that he refers to as "that house"—

himself. Once you see that, you are no longer a prisoner in your own house.

Did my neighbor have any idea that he was not only describing events, but also inventing himself as he told his story?

Awakening and Happiness

"Happiness comes from retiring early."
"Happiness comes from having money and power."
"Happiness comes from getting high on drugs."

Who is this person that you are trying to make happy?

As you get to know her better, your chances of success go up. We have to know someone well in order to be able to make them happy. We have all received birthday presents from people who did not know us very well. Those presents gathered dust on a shelf until we eventually got rid of them. In order to be happy we also need to know our own self well. I know people who retired early with great gusto, only to feel bored and regretful of their choice.

Be Aware of Your Story and Your Style

Notice that all storytellers have a certain style. Hemingway and Groucho Marx would not tell the same story the same way! Shakespeare often has a "fool" come up on the stage and lighten a tragedy.

Notice whether you are a serious dramatist or a variety-show writer who sees the lighter side of things. Notice what your purpose is in telling your story: Is it to elicit pity? To entertain? To convince? To get praise?

Even more important is the effect your story has on *you.*

You can soothe yourself with your story, or you can make yourself feel worse, angrier, and more like a victim—you can make yourself laugh or cry. It all depends on how you tell your story. If the way you tell it is not making you happy, then change the story. Do not give up on your happiness. Give up the story you are telling yourself instead.

Soothing by Changing the Story

Is the toddler crying because her favorite toy broke? Her story is probably, "Poor me. Now I'm forever deprived. My best toy is gone." A parent can change this story by saying something like "We'll get you another one tomorrow" or "We'll glue it together, and you'll see, it will be as good as new." The concept that loss can be repaired, or that it is not the end of the world—it can be tolerated—is a powerful, healing message that we learn from our parents. For loss does not end with childhood, but continues all through life. What changes as we grow older is that now parental soothing must be replaced by self-soothing. Self-soothing creates resilience. Some people rebound quickly after losing a boyfriend or girlfriend, or losing a job. Others get mired in sadness for a long period.

The message of this chapter is that even if self-soothing does not come naturally to you, or if soothing was not your parents' forte, you can still develop self-soothing skills with mindfulness practice. Being able to laugh off adversity, or at least recover from it quickly, is important for a happier life.

Our Parents and Our Storytelling Style

We internalize our parents. We do this spontaneously and without giving any thought to it. We also internalize the soothing style of our parents. If the parent reacts very strongly to minor bruises, that attitude may also be internalized. In this case, rather than feeling soothed, the child—and later on, the adult—may become more agitated.

I encountered this situation recently when Doris, a mother in her fifties, came to see me. Her nineteen-year-old son was still coming to her with every negative emotion he felt, but he was not getting any soothing from her. Instead of soothing him, Doris reacted to Rodney's troubles with acute dismay and distress. This had been a pattern between them. When Rodney was a child, minor aches and pains resulted in trips to the emergency room. Doris recounted that

Rodney actually complained that she overreacted to his moods and made them worse. I was hearing the story of mood contagion, but in the wrong direction, and it had been going on for too long—Rodney was now receiving psychotherapy.

The more usual direction of mood contagion is for *positive feelings* to flow from the mother to the child. But, as I told Doris, we can only give something if we have it. We cannot give what we do not have. Cultivating positive feelings is a necessary skill not only for our own happiness, but also for the happiness of our family and friends.

Happiness as a Duty?

"It is a great mitzvah (commandment) to always be in a state of happiness," said Rabbi Nachman of Breslov, a Hassidic teacher. Indeed, cultivating a joyful spirit is an incitation that runs through many traditional Judaic teachings. Klezmer music and the joyful *niggunim* are testaments to this emphasis on happiness. Itzhak, an Israeli folk dance instructor whom I met in Montreal, was the son of a rabbi, and was deeply steeped in that tradition as a child. He told me that his family used to celebrate the Sabbath by singing all day! In his family even prayer and study were undertaken as joyous activities.

I like to think that a bird gets high not only by flapping its wings, but also by singing. In a song, a bird's whole being vibrates, and becomes joy. We also have the ability to transform our being into sound by singing. We have the same ability to get high and stay high with song. We already have all the equipment we need in order to sing. Just add awareness of this ability and the willingness to use it.

Happiness is the most fragile of the three unalienable rights enshrined in the United States Declaration of Independence—unlike the right to life and liberty, there is no government department charged with protecting this right, and no happiness police. We cannot call 911 if we are not happy. Happiness seems to be such a personal thing that it is easy to assume that a person herself is in charge of her own happiness, and nobody else. Yet, there is no doubt that a parent has the ability to influence her child's happiness level. In the United States, three million children are reported to be abused or neglected each year. Happy people do not abuse their children. Twenty percent of people who were abused by their parents go on to abuse their own children. Statistics say that almost half of all convicted people (not including convictions for traffic violations) were abused as children. If we want to see a happier world, we need to start by finding happiness in our own hearts.

Here is a soul-searching question: Despite that phrase in the constitution, how much do the U.S. government and the various state and municipal governments and governmental institutions, such as the education system, actually do to ensure that citizens are happy?

Self-Soothing by Prayer

"Hail, holy Queen, Mother of Mercy, our life, our sweetness and our hope. To thee do we cry, poor banished children of Eve. To thee do we send up our sighs, mourning and weeping in this valley of tears," goes a Catholic prayer. By saying these verses, the one who is praying evokes the comforting image of the Virgin in her mind.

Devotional soothing is an important part of spiritual traditions. A Catholic finds solace in contemplating the Virgin Mary, and a Muslim finds comfort in considering that no matter how great our sins are, the mercy of Allah is even greater.

The search for soothing is an element in many of our activities. One can look at some kinds of New Age music as lullabies for adults, massage as soothing by appointment, drinking as soothing with alcohol, smoking pot as soothing with cannabis, and recreational eating as soothing with food. Certainly television is often used as a babysitter for children, and even for adults.

Meditation as a Source of Self-Soothing

Thich Nhat Hanh has emphasized the soothing aspect of the practice of mindfulness. In his book *Anger*, he compares anger to a crying baby, and mindfulness to a kind mother who soothes the baby: "The third function of mindfulness is soothing, relieving. Anger is there, but it is being taken care of. The situation is no longer in chaos, with the crying baby left all alone. The mother is there to take care of the baby and the situation is under control." In the following paragraph, he makes the metaphor even more explicit: "And who is this mother? The mother is the living Buddha. The capacity of being mindful, the capacity of being understanding, loving and caring is the Buddha in us."

The soothing power of mindfulness is available to all, regardless of culture or belief. Self-soothing is only one aspect of mindfulness, but it is an important one.

In Buddhist psychology, the seed of mindfulness exists in each of us. We can strengthen our capacity for mindfulness with intentional practice.

Time for Practice

. . . .

Meditation Theme: What Brings You Happiness?

Go through your day mentally. How much happiness does each activity bring you?

If you listen to the radio in the mornings, mentally go through what you hear.

Is it conducive to happiness?

Would you consider listening to something else during some of that time, or just having silence?

Mentally go through the conversations you have with your family, if you live with a family.

How do they usually go? Do they make you happy?

If not, can you envisage different ways of relating to family members, different kinds of conversations?

What can you do to guide those conversations in a better direction?

How does the commute to work play out?

Do you fuss and fume about the slow traffic, or spend that time listening to an inspiring podcast, singing mindfulness songs, or listening to an audiobook?

Each moment of our life is precious. You can prepare for that precious moment on the road beforehand so that it becomes a source of pleasure.

When you arrive at work, are you on the receiving end of the vibes you find there, or are you in touch with your own positive vibes? Do you only complain about the darkness, or do you light a candle?

Do you use reminders to come back to your breath and to your smile during the day? Without reminders, we can easily get caught up in stress. Reminders can range from a BREATHE sign on your computer to a soft mindfulness bell that rings discreetly every twenty-five minutes or so. You can download an app for that.

How do you use your breaks? Are they true breaks, or just interruptions?

Do you ever go out and look at the sky? Do you ever go for a short walk?

When you come back at the end of the day, do you take a few deep breaths and leave behind the day's stress before you enter your house?

If all has gone well for you, remember that the other people you share your life with may not have been so lucky. Can you handle complaints with a smile, without letting them bring you down? Can you instead bring others up?

These are suggestions from my own experience, but they are enough to give you an idea.

We can intentionally change the color of our lives.

Practice Song: Breathe Freely

> Breathe freely, breathe deeply,
> Leave the story behind.

> Sit freely, sit lightly,
> Leave the drama behind.

> In the moment, lighthearted,
> Breathe with a free mind.

The one who breathes,
The one who sits,
Leave them behind.

It is not only when meditating that carrying your story around is problematic. These days, our house is getting a new coat of stucco. I've gotten to know the workers quite well, as from every window I can see them plastering or banging on walls. One of them, André, wanders around with his head down, quite visibly bearing the weight of a lifetime of stories about stories. He takes his drama with him even when he has to walk two steps to pick up something. He is slow as a worker.

Another, Rick, just works. There is lightness to his gestures: when he picks up a hammer, it is just *this* hammer that he is picking up.

No doubt that Rick and André have had different life experiences—so have we all. But remember the definition of mindfulness as "paying attention intentionally." By paying attention intentionally, we can cultivate qualities we find desirable, starting now.

Chapter 3

Go for the Honey

Time for a Story

. . . .

The Wild Strawberry

During the old days when exotic wild animals were not so rare outside the Discovery Channel, a Zen master ran into a tiger one day. The animal snarled and bared its teeth, and the master started to back up. Soon he found himself backed to the edge of a high cliff. The tiger was quite close by now, ready to pounce on him. He looked behind, and saw rocks several hundred feet below. Suddenly he noticed a vine climbing down the chasm, grabbed it with both hands, and swung himself down beyond the reach of the tiger.

As he hung there catching his breath, he noticed that a couple of mice were gnawing on the root of the vine. Tiger above, rocks below, and the vine he was hanging from slowly being chewed up—he was facing certain death.

Suddenly he noticed a bright red wild strawberry to his left. He reached for it and popped it into his mouth. Oh, how sweet it tasted . . .

Time for Reflection

. . . .

The source of a true smile is an awakened mind.
—THICH NHAT HANH

Martin came to a meditation coaching session complaining about his son's problems, and his sadness around the fact that they do not speak to each other anymore. In addition, his wife was not supportive and did not offer him any help or solace. This has been a recurring theme in our meetings, and I try to approach his sadness from different angles so that his meditation practice can be more meaningful for him. On this occasion I started by acknowledging the bittersweet taste of life—suffering is all around us, yet the sweetness of life is also there: the French term *joie de vivre* expresses it well—it is just the joy of being alive, not the joy of being rich or young. By its nature life is a bittersweet mixture, like lemonade.

Making Lemonade

I told Martin that he had just described the lemons, and I asked him where the sweetness in his life came from, where was the honey? To my surprise, he had no idea. He had spent all his time and energy on the lemons, squeezing every drop out of them—he was not prepared for my question.

Bees fly all over meadows and fields, over dead trees, poison ivy, and animal excrement. They do not waste any time wailing over these unsavory things, discussing them in swarms or in the court of Her Majesty, the Queen Bee. They just make a beeline for the flowers, where the sweet nectar is. Then, they come back to the hive and dance in front of other bees to give them the news. Bee news is not about bee crashes or about the mess humans make of things. It is about where the nectar is. It is not about the bitterness of life. It is about its sweetness.

Dukkha or Sukha?

In the Buddhist tradition, Dukkha and Sukha roughly mean Un-happiness and Happiness. These are states of mind, although some writers have imagined them as actual places, much like Heaven and Hell in the Christian tradition. Music is capable of transporting us to one or the other. We can travel to them "On Wings of Song," as the nineteenth-century composer Felix Mendelssohn perceptively put it when he titled one of his songs. By serendipity, Mendelssohn's first name, Felix, means "happy."

Sukha is "unconditional happiness," a little bit like the "unconditional love" that some spiritual texts speak about, because that kind of love does not depend on conditions, or on the Lovability Quotient of the one so loved. It only depends on the state of mind of the lover. If we were lucky, we all thrived on our parents' capacity for unconditional love when we were very young—a howling baby is not particularly lovable, especially at 2 A.M., or when it causes its parents to leave a dinner party before they have eaten.

Imagine not losing your peace of mind and your happy disposition no matter what happens. Imagine always having a loving heart. Some people seem to be like that as a matter of course. Many of us have enjoyed parents who had unconditional happiness, and we grew up in a home that was always a sunny place.

The Buddhist tradition asserts with confidence that we can all develop this trait using the tool of mindfulness, and we can all choose to embark on the path of mindfulness.

There are two basic conditions for finding the unconditional happiness of Sukha:

GO FOR THE HONEY

Being present, and
"Beeing," or going for the honey.

Being present is at the center of Thich Nhat Hanh's teaching—being present not just once in a while, but all the time. And that takes mindfulness. At Plum Village, where he lives, "being here now" is fostered by periodically ringing mindfulness bells, with reminders on the walls, with mindfulness songs, and with the inspiring presence of the residents and of Thich Nhat Hanh himself.

"Beeing" is what the bee does—it is focusing on what is positive, nourishing, and agreeable. In *The Expression of the Emotions in Man and Animals*, Charles Darwin wrote, "The free expression by outward signs of an emotion intensifies it." In other words, the more you yell in anger at someone, the angrier you get.

But on this topic Thich Nhat Hanh goes further. Mindfulness practice considers not only the expression of *outward* signs of emotions, but their *inward* signs as well. The outward signs of anger may be angry words, angry behavior, or an angry face. Inward signs may be rehearsing angry thoughts, brooding with rage, or ruminating with hatred. This kind of covert behavior strengthens our anger, and other negative emotions as well. Anger and mindfulness of anger are two different energies. Mindfulness can soothe the anger. It can create space in the mind so that we can realize that we are more than our anger.

By making us aware of our mental processes, mindfulness makes it possible to have choices. By reminding us constantly of our wish to be happy and to create a happier world, it pushes us each moment to turn our attention around and "water" seeds of positive mental states.

As we become proficient at being more positive and more present, we begin noticing that every day is a beautiful day, for positivity makes us see the beauty in each day. Being in the moment makes it possible to appreciate what is in front of us.

The Nature of Happiness

We are all living on the same Earth—the same sun is shining on all of us, and nature smiles on all of us from every direction. The present moment reveals the Earth in all its splendor. The visions of paradise in literature and religious texts are all memories of our earthly experiences—none of us has actually been there on a cruise and come back with photographs. The vision of happiness in this chapter is not based on denying old age, sickness, loss, and death—but on accepting them. It is strung together with fleeting moments of joy in an impermanent and changing world. It is like the happiness tinged with sadness that we find in Mozart's music, and indeed in all good music. It is happiness on Earth, the only happiness we know. Its bittersweet quality comes from the fact that a taste of sadness is inextricably mixed up with our experience of happiness. In an impermanent world, happiness is a journey, not an end. Trying to amputate all traces of sadness from life would be like trying to make lemonade without the lemons. Without the lemons, we would only have sugar water. Lemons give lemonade its taste, and honey gives it its sweetness.

Applying Wisdom to One's Circumstances

At first, Martin had trouble with the idea of positivity and the concept of "growing happiness." Despite living in a spacious lakefront home with all the creature comforts that come with having a good income, he had trouble identifying positive elements in his life. He had difficulty valuing and appreciating them.

In the end, we agreed on a well-known and well-appreciated routine for the week's daily practice: making a list of things to be grateful for each day. This practice is shared by some positive psychologists.

Allen had a somewhat different challenge. He was assailed by negative thoughts about himself when he tried to meditate. These thoughts had been there before, but they had been manageable. Lately they had been more strident and insistent. He had stopped meditating, because he found it difficult to concentrate through them. He was fighting to keep them at bay, but was unsuccessful in his attempts.

Allen is like a gardener who spends all his effort in fighting weeds. This gardener does not plant any flowers or vegetables. He does not cultivate any desirable plants. He only tries to eradicate undesirable ones. Let us imagine that he is successful. At best, he will only succeed in having an empty lot for a garden—no weeds, but no beautiful or nourishing plants, either. Nothing.

But the nature of mind is like the nature of soil. It is fertile ground. Fill this fertile ground with tasty herbs—plant tomatoes, potatoes, delicious Swiss chard, and sweet basil. Cultivate them. Water and fertilize them. The mental equivalent is positivity meditation. As positive states of mind take root and grow, they take over the mind and crowd out negativity. In any case, our purpose is not to be one hundred percent positive or totally fearless—some amount of fear is necessary for survival.

There is more about gardening and positivity in the next chapter. What you do with your patch of fertile ground is important for your happiness.

❋

In a memorable 1950s song, "Look for the Silver Lining," Judy Garland sang,

> *A heart full of joy and gladness*
> *Will always banish sadness and strife.*

As much as any Zen story from long ago, this song summarizes the journey of this book, because it does not stop with praising what a naturally joyful person spontaneously does. It goes on to reveal the recipe:

> *So always look for the silver lining*
> *And try to find the sunny side of life.*

Fortunately, there's no need to travel far for a glimpse of the sun. Just lift up your head. Use these thoughts as meditation themes. They are both simple and difficult to put into practice at the same time—simple, because they're so obvious, and difficult, because we often forget them. We forget to look up instead of down, and we forget to go deep inside. Instead, we remain on the periphery of the self. There is no need for the tree to go somewhere else to find water. It only needs to reach deep with its roots.

Did everybody who heard Judy Garland's song find lasting happiness? My guess is that most people heard it, smiled with appreciation, and continued to be oppressed by dark clouds as before. Just catching a glimpse of the recipe is not enough. The recipe is not the cake. We must *use* the recipe, *bake* the cake, and *enjoy* it instead.

Time for Practice

. . . .

Practice Theme: "Beeing" Meditation

Visualize an ordinary roadside flower.

We are used to thinking of these flowers as weeds—some, like the dandelion, we even consider a nuisance.

Yet the bee finds honey where we see nuisance. It finds and extracts the honey we fail to see.

There is sunshine in every flower—no sunshine, no flower. There is rain in every flower—no rain, no flower. The bee finds the honey in the sunshine, the rain, the air, and even the earth that we sometimes call "dirt." If someone is cutting trees and turning paradise into a parking lot, the bee does not waste any time bemoaning it. It makes a "beeline" for the flower. Even its eyes are built so that it sees flowers more clearly.

Practice being a bee.

Find honey in every person.

There may be something irritating about the person you are considering.

Many flowers, including the rose, have thorns.

The bee does not dwell on the thorns. It only sees the honey.

Be like the bee.

If that person were a flower and you were a bee, what would you see in her, and how would you act?

Find the honey, and "extract" it for your own nourishment.

Notice that extraction is a proactive process. It does not happen automatically; the bee works at it. The bee is selective. The bee is diligent. The bee is concentrated on the task.

As you bring a person to mind, actually feel the taste of honey in your mouth.

Your boss? She hired you, didn't she? That proves that she has good judgment.

If you are falling out with your romantic partner or with a friend, bring to mind what attracted you to him or her. Remember the honey you found there.

Practice finding the honey in each situation.

Nobody serves the bee a plate of honey. The bee searches for the sweet liquid in each flower and diligently collects the tiny amounts it finds in each flower.

At the end of the day, contemplate and enjoy the honey you also collected.

Practice Song: The Garden Is Now

> *Maybe the most valuable thing I learned from Grandma*
> > *Nelson was that*
> *you can get through hard times if you've got a song in*
> > *your heart.*
> —WILLIE NELSON

The Garden is now, the Garden is here,
In our backyard, or nearer still,
Here has no walls, now has no fear.

Eden is now, Eden is here,
In someone's eyes who shows no fear,
Singing a song, ears cannot hear.

In Eden's choir, all have a voice,
Singing along in the key of life,
The Garden's for all—big, medium, or small,
Not just for Adam and Eve, and their dog . . .

This song suggests that the way we interpret old symbols and images can breathe new life into them. Perhaps we find the mythological story of Paradise not so helpful as it stands. As it is, that story says that the Earth is not Paradise; it is a vale of tears. This song turns that old attitude on its head: Paradise is here and now, not somewhere else.

If we take that to heart, we end up appreciating the uniqueness and the preciousness of our life here, in each moment.

The old story says that some outside force expelled us from the Garden. The new story says that we lost the Garden as we lost our freshness and our presence. The Garden is a state of mind, not a physical place. We can go back there by using the two practices outlined in this chapter—mindfulness and positive thinking.

This is an empowering vision.

The story of the Garden is rich in its implications, and is of central importance if we are to bring ourselves to see the Earth as the only paradise there is.

Chapter 4

Cultivate the Garden
of Your Heart

Time for a Story

....

Buddha's Garden

A meditation student asked:

"What does the Buddha do when he is meditating?"

"He cultivates the Garden of his Heart" was the answer.

"How does he do it?" the student pursued.

"By watering and nourishing the beautiful flowers that grow there—flowers like love, compassion, and serenity," replied the teacher.

"When will he be finished with that job?"

"A garden is never finished," said the teacher. "That's why the Buddha is still meditating in all his pictures and statues."

Time for Reflection

. . . .

Take your time.
Everything happens at its own pace.
The gardener may water with a hundred buckets,
But the fruit ripens only in season.
—KABIR

Steps Toward Positivity

The Buddhist model for moving toward positivity is "Cultivating the garden of the heart."

It uses the organic model of gardening. When we garden, we water, fertilize, and take care of plants that are nourishing or beautiful. We fill our garden with those plants, and we help them grow. In this model, we see the Buddha as a gardener. In fact, he is both a garden and a gardener: there is a garden in his heart.

I sit with statuettes of the Buddha and of Quan Yin, the "Female Buddha" as she is called in Chinese gift shops. Quan Yin is the bodhisattva of compassion, and having them together on my altar establishes gender equality and gender harmony—and, if I'm sitting with others, it allows the women in the group to focus on a being with whom they can relate more naturally. There are also flowers around, and a handwritten sign that says BUDDHA'S GARDEN. The two Buddhas in front of me have been cultivating the garden of their hearts for many centuries, and I join them. Now we are doing this together.

The psychological model is "positivity meditation."

This involves bringing to mind things to be grateful for, es-

pecially at night before going to sleep. Do not stop with gratitude, however. Also consider things to hope for, things to be glad
about . . . You can copy the list of positive emotions below and put it
somewhere within sight:

Joy
Gratitude
Gladness
Serenity
Interest, engagement
Hope
Pride (a feeling more like self-esteem than haughtiness)
Amusement
Inspiration
Awe or wonder (such as in front of nature)
Love (includes compassion, friendliness, kindness, and
  sympathy)
Contentment
Confidence
Admiration
Appreciation

Read this list out loud once a day. It helps to have a clear notion
of where you want to go. Often when I ask for a list of negative emotions, people have no trouble blurting out "anger, fear, hatred . . ."
When I ask for a list of positive emotions, the list emerges much
more slowly. Sometimes, there are long silences between words.

Fill your heart with these positive emotions. When negative
emotions pop up in your mind, do not dwell on them. Dwell on
their positive counterparts.

I have learned that some people relate better to one model or the
other.

Elsie was a successful lawyer, and I thought she would relate
better to the psychological, "scientific" aspect of positivity medita-

tion because of her professional training. I was wrong. Elsie did not enjoy the idea of positivity. She complained that it felt artificial to her, and contrary to her nature. She felt she was trying to be Polly-anna, and it went against the grain. So I changed my tack. I asked her if she had any houseplants. She said, "Yes." I then asked her if she kept poison ivy, thorns, or crabgrass for houseplants. She looked at me from the corner of her eye, and said, "No." She had no trouble accepting the fact that the existence of noxious weeds did not mean that we had to cultivate them at home. Similarly, when we decide to cultivate the garden of our heart, we are cultivating an intimate space, and we take care to put what brings us happiness in that space. Only after that space is blooming can we succeed in giving others a "contact high." Changing the world has to start by chang-ing ourselves, and that starts by changing our most intimate space—our heartspace.

Positive or Positively Annoying?

The gardening metaphor for cultivating positive traits has a subtlety that is missing in the kind of positivity that is promoted in pop psy-chology. Although I consider him a pioneer of positive psychology, no one can accuse Buddha of being a rah-rah kind of pop psycholo-gist. Buddha is an organic gardener—the flowers of positivity in his garden have grown slowly by a natural process without artificial fer-tilizers. In contrast, the other kind of positivist may have a flashy side—she may even express it by wearing flamboyant clothes and talking loudly. Her positivity may even be fueled by drugs. The feel-ing tone may be quite different. The personality type, whether the person is an introvert or an extrovert at heart, also makes a differ-ence in how feelings are expressed.

There is some movement toward positivity in a stress reduction course—negativity makes stress worse. There is also an element of positivity in meditation training as I offer it. Working with cancer patients involves a bolstering of attitude as well. Yet, I have learned to go slowly when guiding people toward positivity. It takes time for flowers to grow—this is true of botanical as well as metaphoric flowers. Going too fast creates resistance. Some people are simply allergic to anything that feels facile or superficial to them.

The metaphor of cultivating the garden of our heart is far reaching. We water the seeds of positive states of mind not only with our thoughts, but also with our feelings, words, and actions. Every conversation, every song we listen to, every video we watch is an act of watering seeds—seeds of poison ivy or seeds of lavender. We also water seeds with the way we drive, the way we walk or clean the house—we water seeds of impatience and discontent, or of peace and contentment.

Wanting Quick Results

Impatience is the enemy of a successful meditation practice.

I have met people who had been practicing unproductive mental habits for decades, but wanted meditation to help change them overnight. Or people who have been on psychotherapeutic drugs for years without much change in outlook, and wanted meditation to work in a few weeks.

These people would be unhappy with a small, one percent change over a week. They might not even notice it. But do not underestimate one percent. One percent a week works out to a hundred percent over two years. This means a complete change can be made in a couple of years. In contrast, it took Buddha six years to make such a thoroughgoing change in his outlook and lifestyle.

Organic change is like a tree growing, or a garden blooming. It is not instant.

Notice the two elements of stilling and hearing in the following quote by Thich Nhat Hanh:

> When you've been able to still all the noise inside of you, when you've been able to establish silence, a thundering silence, in you, you begin to hear the deepest kind of calling from within yourself. Your heart is calling out to you.

Do not stop with the first part, the stilling. Go on to the second part, the listening.

Cultivating the garden of your heart makes the song that comes from inside more like a birdsong that is full of the wonder of the universe.

Feelings are not thoughts. They do not have to make sense.

Sometimes, they pull in one direction, while our thoughts pull in another.

Sometimes the thoughts lead; sometimes the feelings lead and thoughts follow.

All the same, our peace of mind demands that we reconcile them—we need this reconciliation, for when the time comes to act, we need to go one way or the other and we need to go in one piece. Finding peace is the work of wholeness, the work of becoming *one*.

Without doing this work, we are prey to what psychologists call *cognitive dissonance*. We vacillate. We may ignore our feelings and follow the mind. Or follow the mind, and suffer pangs of conscience.

The remedy? Meditate. Spend some time with yourself. Become intimate with yourself.

Know yourself.

Awareness of Emotions

Emotions can be like sunglasses, and our different emotions like the different-colored sunglasses on the drugstore rack. When we are suffused with hope and joy, it is as if we are wearing pink-colored glasses. When we are under the sway of anxiety and sadness, gray-colored ones. Things *look* different depending on our emotional state or mood, and if we do not know our emotional state, we might think that the world itself is a gloomy place, or the person we are looking at is a true villain.

Emotions can also turn time into an elastic band—an elastic band that shortens when we are having a good time, and stretches with impatience or boredom.

Becoming aware of our emotional states allows us to see things as they are, and the world as it is. It allows us to compensate for the sunglasses we may be wearing.

Emotions: The Color of Life

The delicate carpet of flowers in a meadow, the garden of corals under the ocean, and the industrious life of bees and ants all take place against a backdrop of weather, of calm sunny days as well as menacing dark clouds, rain, fog, thunder, lightning, storms, hurricanes, frost, and the occasional earthquake. The human world is a bit more complicated than the natural world, as, for us, the "weather" also includes our internal weather—the storms and the rest happen not only out there, but inside us as well.

The meditator is like a gardener, weeding, nourishing, and watering the garden. She does this against the backdrop of the events of her life.

Stages of Emotion

An emotion can happen without our awareness. That is the first level. Our heart rate and blood pressure may rise without yet piercing through our awareness to make us *feel* anger, for example.

The word "feeling" refers to the second level, when we have subjective awareness of an emotion. Before this level, an emotion is not necessarily articulated or named. This is a nebulous state that can give rise to confusion, or inspire a poem as in the following verse by the Peruvian poet Manuel González Prada:

> Your eyes are saying something
> But what they are saying, I do not know.

Here the poet is describing a certain level of ambiguity inherent in emotions.

My understanding of that verse is that the owner of those eyes herself has probably not yet verbalized her feelings. This is a tricky state where we can act out a feeling, or become emotional or moody like a teenager sometimes is. The poet here is describing a person who can hold a feeling in her heart without doing either—much like Mona Lisa seems to do in the celebrated painting by Leonardo da Vinci. No one has yet figured out what she was feeling in all these years.

Many psychotherapists recommend moving into the third stage, where we label our emotions and feeling states. By doing that, it is easier to "get a handle" or "get a grip" on our emotions. The German word for concept (*Begriff*) is related to the word for a handle (*Griff*). It is easier to deal with things that have handles.

However, there are many more colors in nature than we have words for. This is also true of feelings. A feeling is different from the label we assign to it. Also, like the colors of a sunset, or the colors of a flower that change as the light changes, our feelings also change from moment to moment.

Naming Emotions

Naming an emotion is taming it. Naming brings the raw, wordless emotion that comes from the more primitive regions of the brain into the sphere of the frontal cortex, into the living room of the mind. It brings light into the turbulence emotions often create. If emotion is the weather, naming it is like the weather report.

It is recommended for the clarity it brings into our feelings.

Ideally, as we name an emotion, we know it both as a feeling and also understand it conceptually. The DailyWritingTips.com website lists seventy-five words for different shades of anger. They range from aggravated to bitter, from furious to ticked-off. I think that if I were angry, and you read me the whole list and asked me to pick the word that best expresses my feeling, I might burst out laughing and forget about the anger I'm feeling. That is the advantage of naming. You go from being the one who has the baby to being the one who is trying to pick a name for it. Naming distracts you from the baby by turning your attention to christening it.

Emotions Do Not Always Fit into a Box

What are my feelings about the state of our beautiful planet Earth, and the environmental wounds we are inflicting on her every day? I feel *sadness*, but also *anger* toward certain corporations and governments that are twisting the knife in her wounds with particular cruelty. I feel *disappointment* that we are missing such a precious opportunity to leave a clean environment to our children. I feel *longing* for a better future for them. I feel *gratitude* that I live in a part of the world (Québec) that still has a relatively clean environment. I feel *irritation* that the scientists who tell us that our environmental practices are unsustainable and the governments and corporations that make the decisions seem to live in different worlds. I feel *outraged* at the dishonesty of certain corporations and politicians who twist facts for self-serving reasons.

I'm listing them separately, but are these emotions really separate? It seems to me that they are more like one big Rubik's Cube with different-colored sides. Looking at the cube, I see many colors at the same time: sadness for what we are doing to the Earth, delight in waking up to a bright sunny day, and hope that perhaps, somehow, we will get wiser and develop a more caring attitude.

"I have mixed feelings," we sometimes say. Indeed, it looks to me as if mixed feelings are the rule rather than the exception. Just bring to mind your feelings toward your job or your boyfriend or girlfriend!

Perhaps if you encountered a fierce tiger when you stepped out of your front door, you'd come as close as you ever would to a pure feeling: that of fear. But then, there may also be an element of surprise in it—a different feeling . . .

Naming an emotion puts it into a box, and in a sense, words are boxes.

But try putting beauty into a box. Or life.

Boxing living things denatures them in subtle ways, and feelings are living things.

Expressing Emotions

One can express an emotion without trapping it in words. One can express it in music, dance, poetry, or art. We do not reduce an emotion to "ideas about an emotion" when we express it creatively. The artistic expression of an emotion is embodied. The dancer is a body, not a concept. So is a singer. Expressing an emotion artistically does not denature it. It puts it out there in such a way that others can also feel it. As opposed to labeling, expressing an emotion in a creative way does not conceptualize it. It presents a feeling as a feeling.

In order to do that well, one must feel and contain an emotion nonverbally. One must also have the tools to express it directly in a creative way rather than explain it discursively, as a dictionary or an encyclopedia would.

We often think of eyes as windows to the outside world, but they are also windows to the world inside. In the example of Prada's poem on page 53, the *eyes* are expressing the feelings, and not words. Words would be labeling them instead.

Acting Out Emotions

In acting out emotions, there is a direct line from emotion to action. The emotional brain is given a free hand, and there is usually not much input from other brain regions.

However, we are not only our emotions. Acting emotionally disregards the rest of our brain, and reduces us to our emotional impulses.

Anger or aggressiveness is often associated with acting out.

Two Ways of Being Emotional

"Emotional" has two meanings in the dictionary that do not necessarily go together. One is having emotions, being aware of them, and valuing them. An "emotional farewell" and "emotional intelligence" are examples of the use of the word in this positive sense.

The other is behavior that is based on emotion rather than reason. This sense, in contrast, is felt to be negative. Buddha was more aware of his emotions than most of us, female or male, but he was not emotional in the second sense.

"Emotional" can be a demeaning label, because it implies that we use emotions rather than intelligence to navigate through life, just like animals and young children do. Road rage is being emotional. So is domestic violence. Both are more common among men than among women.

"Being emotional" and "being aware of one's emotions" are more often opposites than cognates. A Doberman baring its teeth at you, or a toddler crying because another child took away one of her toys, are both acting out their feelings without awareness. Awareness creates space in the mind: there is emotion, but there is also mindfulness—two different mental energies. The space that awareness creates is part of the stuff of emotional intelligence.

Time for Practice

. . . .

Guided Meditation: Cultivating Positive States of Mind

Contentment is natural wealth.

—SOCRATES

This exercise starts out as contemplation, and ends as a meditation.

Contemplating the sources of positive emotions brings happiness.

At the end of the contemplation, spend some time sitting in that state—it is like basking in the sun.

Take a few deep breaths,
and get in touch with all the physical sensations of breathing.
Concentrate on the breath
until you feel your breath becoming slow and regular.

❧

Bring to mind three sources of contentment.
  What makes you content?
Look deeper if you only find discontent.
Hint: Contentment is about what we already have.
  Discontent is about what we lack.

❊

What brings you joy?
Bring to mind two or three sources of joy from earlier today or
*   yesterday.*
Savor them for a few moments now.

❊

What makes you glad? What brings gladness?
Did you go through your day or your week without feeling
*   gladness?*
Go back in your experience, and look again.
*   Find some sources of gladness, and dwell on them briefly.*
Hint: Joy is more exuberant. Gladness is a quieter feeling,
*   a feeling of being pleased.*

❊

Contemplate the miracle of breathing,
*   the miracle of being alive.*
Feel the mystery of how life was transmitted to you.
Feel the richness of just being alive.
Hint: This is the feeling of wonder—
*   almost of reverence for something bigger;*
something we do not quite comprehend.

❊

Find gratitude in your heart—
*   for a teacher, a mentor, your parents,*
or whoever helped make you into what you are now.
Gratitude can also be for having eyes that see,
*   or legs to walk on—*
not everybody is so fortunate.

❋

Dwell on love.
Visualize your loved ones, and fill your heart with loving
*   feelings for them.*
Fill your heart with loving feelings for yourself,
for the beautiful child you were, and for the beautiful person
*   you are now.*

❋

Continue sitting for a few extra moments, immersed in the
positive energies stirred up by this exercise.

Practice: Shower Someone with Appreciation

In this practice, we are helping to cultivate someone else's garden.

Pick someone close to you, and for two or three weeks, shower her with compliments and appreciative comments. When I suggested this in a group, one participant commented to general laughter: "My mother-in-law will be quite surprised this week!" The person you choose can also be a child, a parent, or a work colleague. However, be careful in your choice so that your positive comments will not be interpreted as flirting.

After a few weeks notice the change in the quality of your relationship with this person.

Chapter 5

Don't Get in Your Own Way

Time for a Story

. . . .

Flow Like a River

During a T'ai Chi class one day, the master noticed that one of his students was moving awkwardly. When he was practicing alone, his gestures did not flow. When he was practicing with others, he had trouble handling the energy of his sparring partner. The presence of the other person made him stiff and rigid.

"Come with me," said the master, and took him to a stream in the woods nearby.

"To move freely and effectively, you must understand harmony. Look at the stream. There are rocks in its way. Does it stop flowing when they get in its way? No. Does it slam into them out of frustration? No. It simply flows over and around them and moves on. Be like the water and you will know what harmony is."

The young man sat by the flowing stream for a long while.

When he returned to the practice hall, the song of the stream was still in his ears.

Time for Reflection

....

<blockquote>
Yield and win,
Bend and stay straight,
Be empty so you can be full,
Let go, and be renewed,
Have little, and be rich,
Have much and be confused.

—TAO TE CHING (#22)
</blockquote>

Humans are a funny lot. Some cripple themselves with obesity while others starve themselves with anorexia. These behaviors are examples of people getting in their own way, as no one else is forcing them to make themselves miserable. They are doing it all by themselves.

Here are some other unskillful mental and emotional ways in which people also get in their own way. If you find yourself somewhere on the following pages, quickly extricate yourself from there.

Driving with the Brakes On

The car has a gas pedal and a brake pedal. You use the gas pedal when you want to go somewhere. You use the brake pedal when you arrive where you want to go. If you want to go someplace, take your foot off the brake.

If you have a dream or a goal such as a job, a university degree, or a house you would like to have, but you keep your foot on the brake pedal of hesitations and fears, you will not realize your goal.

Every car has those pedals. Every one of us has hesitations and fears. They prevent us from speeding on the road, from engaging in unprotected or inappropriate sex, and sometimes they even prevent us from cheating on our income tax. Do not use the gas pedal in those circumstances. Use the gas pedal when you are dreaming of a job that you are qualified for. Use it when you have met a person you like, and that you would like to get to know better. Use it when opportunity winks at you. In those circumstances, go as fast as the speed limit allows—do not dawdle. Don't even think of the brakes.

We get in our own way when we keep our foot on the brake pedal all the time.

Why do we do this when it is obviously a self-defeating thing to do? We do it because of self-doubt, fear, shyness, low self-image, reticence, procrastination, hesitation, being unsure of ourself, all of the above, or a mix of some of the above.

The gas pedal and the brake pedal are not meant to get in each other's way. They are meant to work together to help the driver navigate through her life successfully. If you feel your hope, your enthusiasm, and your life force reaching toward something, and you are stopping yourself, it is time to go to a meditation retreat. Choose a retreat where there is an opportunity for private interviews. Take advantage of the opportunity and open up. Negative mental states such as fears dissolve during meditation as we see through them—the thrust of meditation practice is toward being the *observer* of our mental states. Meditation moves us toward greater awareness.

Never Satisfied

We talk about self-made people. But there are also a great many self-destroyed people. Here are two larger-than-life examples we are all familiar with: Saddam Hussein and Moammar Gadhafi. These dictators brought on their own demise by overreaching. It is true that outside force was also used to bring them down, but these men made that outside force necessary by their own unwise actions. This is just the tip of the iceberg. Think of lesser-known politicians who have brought on their own demise. A top golfer we all know for whom one woman, his wife, was not enough. Celebrities and others who have ruined their lives through addiction. And as the ultimate example of self-destruction, think of suicide—the second leading cause of death among college students. The thread that runs through these examples is a lack of satisfaction with life.

Self-Sabotage

We "make" ourselves, our relationships, and careers—but we also destroy them. We often mess up our relationships with parents, children, and siblings. We get jobs, but sometimes we also sabotage the jobs we worked hard to get. We sabotage friendships, and we sabotage our own happiness.

"People have a hard time letting go of their suffering. Out of a fear of the unknown, they prefer suffering that is familiar." When I read that quotation by Thich Nhat Hanh to Gisele, there was an immediate look of recognition on her face. "Yep, that's me," she said.

I was glad that my hunch was correct: there was a reason why I had chosen to read her that quote. We had been going over the same terrain for several months in our meetings, without any change on her part. At the end of each session, she seemed to be on the edge of a breakthrough, but at the beginning of the next session she would come back with the same complaints and the same outlook as if nothing had ever happened. Conscious recognition did not lead to beneficial change for Gisele. She continued to come back with the same issues for many subsequent meetings. She was not practicing very often between her sessions with me.

Positivity needs to become a habit rather than just a wish if it is to make a change in one's happiness level. Repetition is the food on which habits thrive.

Addiction is not too strong a word for clinging to feelings with which we are familiar. I recommended a meditation retreat to her. It would serve the same purpose as a residential treatment for addiction. When on her own, Gisele would likely return to her old ways of thinking and feeling. In a residential retreat, she would not be on her own.

Here is another story: "My boss did a number of silly things. She accused me of trying to make out with a sales rep, and offering her discounts in order to score with her. She kept pointing out every little mistake I made with clients. But now that I look back on it, I see that I made the situation worse by throwing oil on the fire. I responded to her threats by working harder. This had the opposite effect on her. She saw me as a competitor for her job, and got scared. I don't know why I did not just sit down and have a good talk with her." Paul had just quit a well-paying job out of exhaustion. Now unemployed, he had plenty of time to think about his last months at work.

Solange, another client, had had a bitter argument with her boyfriend the previous week. In talking about it, she saw clearly that it was his fault. But she also realized that she made things worse by how she reacted, and had a hand in the argument escalating to relationship-shaking proportions. She had been defensive and critical, more so than she realized at the time.

These are all examples of people getting in their own way.

Poor diet, smoking, and drinking more than is good for us are other examples. According to the WHO, up to 80 percent of chronic illnesses are self-inflicted. Sure, health challenges, difficult working conditions, unreasonable bosses, and relationship troubles have a way of happening without help from us. But in many cases, we make these issues worse by the way we react, or by our lifestyle choices.

Striving Too Hard

The Chinese sage Mencius tells the story of a foolish farmer who thinks that his sprouts are not growing fast enough. He pulls on them to make them grow faster. At the end of the day he comes home and tells his son that he feels quite tired, because all day long he was helping plants grow. When the son hears that, he rushes out to the greenhouse to have a look, and sees that his fears are confirmed—the plants are all damaged or dead.

Mencius contrasts this with growing seeds the natural way—all we have to do is make sure that they are covered with soil, water them, and do some weeding. They will do just fine.

Thich Nhat Hanh is echoing Mencius's prescription when he advocates growing happiness by watering the seeds of positive emotions. He often elaborates on the gardening metaphor by mentioning the organic nature of this process, how manure and compost (our negative emotions) are transformed in the process into lovely flowers or nourishing plants.

In line with Mencius's metaphor, I can think of a number of nonorganic shortcuts for trying to force happiness to grow. Chief among them are alcohol, substance abuse, and compulsive shopping.

The first of Buddha's Four Noble Truths is that wherever humans are, there is some amount of unhappiness, stress, and suffering. That is not all there is, but those factors are present from time to time. It looks to me as if today, just like in Buddha's day, there is an unwillingness to accept that adversity, suffering, or stress are part of life. We see these as "mistakes" that should not occur, and we want them fixed. According to the statistics compiled by the Centers for Disease Control, nearly half the U.S. population is on at least one prescription drug. According to Dr. Mehmet Oz, that proportion is 70 percent. Painkillers are the most prescribed medicines. Number three on the list are antidepressants.

In this book I will outline another outlook based on acceptance. That outlook does not say, "Just suck it up and suffer." On the contrary.

It is a proactive outlook that says, "Grow up; develop resilience, mood regulation, and all the other skills mentioned in the Table of Contents and described in detail in the text." As you do that, you will notice a change in attitude. Happiness and wisdom go hand in hand.

This raises a question for public health and education administrators: If a majority among us need psychotropic medicines just to go through life and bear its adversities, isn't it time to consider including mindfulness education in our public school curriculum as an essential subject?

Searching for Happiness with Pills

The United States is the only country that allows pharmaceutical companies to advertise their products directly to the consumer. In true advertising fashion, the benefits of these drugs are exaggerated. People are already well disposed toward taking them. Who wouldn't like to just take a pill, have all their problems solved, and feel deliriously happy ever after? Physicians oblige their unhappy patients and try to help. Eighty percent of psychotropic drugs are prescribed by pediatricians and family physicians who have had insufficient training in psychiatry or psychotherapy. Here is a personal example: When she was three or four, my daughter was prescribed Valium by her pediatrician because she regularly woke up screaming in the middle of the night. We refused to fill that prescription, and did some investigating. We finally traced her problems to her daycare—she was served a sugary drink, sweet cookies, and lollipops every afternoon. We asked that the sweets be discontinued, and starting from the first day, she slept through the night. Widely fluctuating blood sugar levels play havoc with our moods, at any age.

There are similar lifestyle solutions to many problems.

Job Conditioning

The practice of acceptance has many twists and turns.

We must first accept what is there before fixing it—even when it needs fixing. Otherwise our wish to fix things can get in the way.

Leanne was a chiropractor, and like some other people in the helping professions, she had "become" her professional self—she was helpful twenty-four hours a day! This was driving her boyfriend crazy—he could not do or say anything without being "helped" with an avalanche of suggestions and comments. Leanne had become the ultimate Mr. Fixit that John Gray talks about in his book *Men Are from Mars, Women Are from Venus*. My experience with the "Mr.

Fixit syndrome" is that it is not so much a gender-based phenomenon anymore. It is now what the French call a *déformation professionnelle*— a job conditioning that comes from assuming your professional role in your private life.

I did a role-playing exercise with Leanne. I would say things like "I broke my leg," and she had to respond with "Is that so?" No suggestions about calling an ambulance, icing the leg, or running out to get painkillers. Just, "Is that so?" At first this sounded strange to her. But soon she got into the play and was responding, "Is that so?" with gusto to my assumed complaints such as "I have a cold" or "I think I'm suffering from depression." She had gotten the point.

Acceptance, empathy, and connection are preludes to helping. Fixing without those qualities is not always about helping somebody— it is often about gratifying the ego of the fixer. The fixer "knows." The poor uninformed one, the one with the problem, doesn't.

While identities such as "Problem Solver" or "Mr. Fixit" may work in the limited context of our professional lives, they are less appropriate in the limitless context of our personal lives. How do you "solve" aging, degenerative illnesses, and death? Those, and many others like loss and disappointment, are universal human experiences. They need empathy and acceptance. Problem solving works better after those are given. Acceptance is expressed by listening, and by the quality of the listening. Often it is just an acknowledgment of our common humanity. This puts the fixer and the fixed on an equal footing.

You can get in your own way when you take your job conditioning home with you.

You enrich your work life when you bring a piece of your humanity with you to work.

Can't Stop Butting Heads

I just read a report of a $2 billion settlement for the NFL players who have suffered concussions as a result of high-speed collisions on the field. My mind went back to those National Geographic movies where mountain goats, bighorn sheep, deer, bison, moose, antelope, and musk oxen butt heads in order to intimidate each other and establish superiority. There's even a species of fish that does it. We have evolved since those days, but it looks like our old ways are still with us: head injury is a big issue among hockey players and boxers as well as football players.

It appears that as humans evolved, we added on some traits, such as intelligence, without taking away others, such as head butting. Granted that some of us have moved it from the literal to the metaphorical level—we now mostly do it in arguments. We do it in a formalized way in the judicial or the political arenas; we do it informally with our spouses and teenage children, and in the workplace with our coworkers. I've even known people who butt heads all by themselves—their usual tone of musing is one of arguing, even if nobody is arguing with them.

In the animal kingdom there are winners and losers in the head-butting match. That is how evolution works. But among humans, head butting only creates losers—both the winner and the loser get concussions. This is also true to some extent in metaphorical head butting—as a wife and husband ram heads, both of them suffer. As a father and son do it, they both bleed in their hearts. But they usually do not know how to stop. Those spiraling and unwieldy horns we see on musk oxen have become invisible with evolution, but they are still there, getting in our way as we move around. Be aware of them—of your own, as well as those of others'. Speak mindfully and with kindness in your heart.

More on Mindful Communication

"If you do not ask for help when you need it, you are not kind," say the Nootka, an indigenous tribe of British Columbia. Yet, when what someone does or says makes us unhappy, we do everything except ask for help. We fuss and fume, sulk, stay awake at night, and sometimes explode with anger.

In the older tribal consciousness, our oneness was deeply ingrained in the consciousness. Now, we are more aware of our separateness and individuality. Communication has a different flavor when you assume that everybody is on the same side—asking for help feels more natural.

Compassion is a feeling we have for people who are on the same side as us.

As we cultivate compassion, we begin to see everyone as being on the same side, in the same family, in the same spaceship.

Begin with the feeling of compassion, or the point of view of inclusion. Either is fine as a starting point. What we say and how we say it has the potential to make others happy or unhappy. Whether we go around sowing happiness or unhappiness in turn affects our own happiness—it affects how others see us and treat us.

I know only too well that having tasted peace is not the same as being able to speak from a peaceful place every time I open my mouth. In communication, we are affected by the state of mind of the person we are addressing. Remaining peaceful in the presence of the emotions of another requires us to be firmly rooted in peace *and* compassion.

Getting Stuck at the Verbal Level

In her book *A Man without Words*, Susan Schaller describes the journey of Ildefonso, a twenty-seven-year-old deaf man learning sign language. Being deaf from birth, Ildefonso has no concept of language as a means of communication. When Schaller signs to him, he simply imitates her. When she signs, "I'm Susan," he signs back, "I'm Susan." He lives in a silent world without words, and takes her signs simply as gestures to imitate.

One morning, this man had a breakthrough, and realized, "Everything has a name."

"He had joined the human race," remarks Schaller. When she contacted him some years later and asked for his recollections of his pre-language days, he did not remember anything—in those days he lived in a world of silence. How much do we remember from the time before we discovered language as young children?

That time was an experience-based world. The world is still experience-based, but we relate to it largely through symbols—through those names that everything has. This has made communication possible, but it has also made us vulnerable to superficiality, as it has contracted the meaning of things and living beings to their labels. It has made the restaurant menu almost the equivalent of the reality of a tasty dish. For many people it has made ideology and philosophy a substitute for wisdom, and made it easier for us to be seduced by words—by politicians' promises, by the hype of advertising, and even by religious promises of heaven.

It is interesting that both Susan Schaller and Oliver Sacks, who wrote the foreword to her book, allude to Ildefonso's pre-language personality as Adam. Adam tasted the fruit of the tree of knowledge, and was exiled from Paradise. Do we really want to go back to a silent Paradise? Many people think that their purpose in taking up meditation is to silence the mind. But do we really want that? Ildefonso did not. He was grateful to have discovered language, and resentful that he did not discover it sooner.

Language and language-based thinking are not the real culprits, however. The mindfulness deficit that allows us to be slaves to language and its reductionist ways is the problem. Can we use language instead of being used by it? Can we have a taste of silence every once in a while, and discover the source from which our words come? For we need them both—we need both the silence and the words.

Being Disconnected from the Heart

We watch all the violence going on in the world on television. We even know in our hearts the roots of it: cruelty, ideology, an inability to listen and consider the point of view of others. But we may unwittingly do the same things ourselves on a smaller scale when we communicate.

The Buddhist tradition that gave rise to the practice of mindfulness suggests a radical transformation of our motivation. It suggests that we always keep in mind kindness, open-mindedness, and a willingness to listen and understand. As we practice always acting and speaking from the heart, many of the self-created obstacles on our path disappear.

❧

Being and Doing

Education enhances our doing.

Meditation enhances our being, our natural qualities.

Education adds. It adds to our knowledge—it adds to what we can do.

Meditation subtracts. It subtracts layers of illusion.

What you put on your résumé is your *doing*. The reason why employers also want a face-to-face interview is because they want to get a sense of your *being*. Intimate relationships are about being. You fall in love with—or at least you are taken by—a person's being. Work life and employment are about doing. People hire you for what you can *do*. In contrast, people want to share your life for who you *are*.

We go to school, and we develop marketable skills. We value the success they bring. But do not underestimate *being*. We get cats and dogs, and spend much time and energy looking after them, not because of anything they do, but because we enjoy what they are—their presence enriches our life. We adore babies and children for the same reason. Their being adds meaning to our life. We enjoy nature, flowers, birds, and butterflies for their being and their presence.

When your actions are a direct result of your true nature, they happen naturally, without undue effort on your part. The harder you try to sleep, the more sleep eludes you. If you just get out of your own way, and let things take their course, sleep comes more easily. This is also one of the recipes for achieving flow—flow in music, dance, conversation, and in just plain living.

As we come closer to awakening, our being and our doing also edge closer toward each other. Can you tell them apart in Buddha's life?

Time for Practice

. . . .

Meditation Theme: "Thank You" Meditation

Most meditators complain that their mind has a tendency to overthink. Simon, an elderly gentleman who attended one of my groups, even went so far as to declare that he wanted to stop thinking. I gently pointed out to him that this was not a very good goal, for if he succeeded in it, he might not be able to find his way back home. A better goal would be to slow this runaway train or, better still, to hire a conductor to manage its speed. However, a conductor needs some training. Imagine yourself at the controls of a speeding train, and you have no idea which lever to push to slow it down!

Well, you are that conductor. Now it's time for some on-the-job training. "Thank You" meditation is one way.

First, take a few minutes to convince yourself that you are not your brain. You are not just three pounds of Jell-O, a Humpty Dumpty without arms or legs, without eyes, without a heart, and without skin.

The brain tries to convince you that you are. The following conversation from *Alice in Wonderland* is a good metaphor:

"I don't know what you mean by 'glory,'" Alice said.

Humpty Dumpty smiled contemptuously. "Of course you don't—till I tell you. I meant 'there's a nice knock-down argument for you!'"

"But 'glory' doesn't mean 'a nice knock-down argument,'" Alice objected.

"When I use a word," Humpty Dumpty said, in rather a scornful tone, "it means just what I choose it to mean—neither more nor less."

"The question is," said Alice, "whether you can make words mean so many different things."

"The question is," said Humpty Dumpty, "which is to be master—that's all."

This passage describes the problem well. The brain decides what things mean, and considers itself the master. But sometimes *it* is the problem. We need a conductor. Instead, we sometimes get a runaway train—a "train brain."

Take charge, and be the master. Mentally say "Thank You" every time the brain offers you a thought. "Thank You, Thank You, Thank You." Stand your ground, even when you *like* the thought your brain offers. This "Thank You" is a polite way of refusing to play its game. Do not argue. Just say "Thank You" every time you hear a thought, and do not get involved. This is a great way to train yourself to dissociate from the voice of the brain.

I suggest three such ten-minute meditation sessions on different days.

Soon, each thought will spontaneously evoke a "Thank You" response.

Practice Song: My Heart Is at Ease

Think of this song as a song for tuning your heart's strings.

> *My heart is at ease, my mind at peace,*
> *In Earth's green garden, here and now.*
> *Awake or in a dream, life flows like a stream*
> *In Earth's green garden, here and now.*

A few words about the "dream" in the third line.

"This place is a dream. Only a sleeper considers it real," said Rumi.

"A man that is born falls into a dream like a man who falls into the sea," wrote Joseph Conrad.

What exactly did they mean?

This song comes out of my own experience. Recently I was in Montreal wearing several layers of clothing against the bitter winter cold, and the next day I found myself in a boat surrounded by dolphins in a remote corner of the Pacific coast of Mexico. As I gazed across the blue ocean, I had the strong feeling that I was in a dream.

It is my sensory experience that defines the world for me, and I consider my sensory experience to be "reality." But dolphins, bees, and birds do not see the same world. It is being aware of this that suffuses the world I'm in with the magic charm of a dream. In a way, we are all in a dream—there are at least as many dreams as there are species in the world, and, according to a recent estimate, there are 8.7 million of them. What the Buddhist tradition calls *samsara* also means "going through life without awareness of its dreamlike quality." In this sense, the metaphor of waking up, or awakening, is not what happens when the alarm rings; it is what happens when the meditation bell rings.

This understanding has practical applications: we are in a different dream when we are in love than when we are out of love—we see the world differently depending on our emotional state.

Chapter 6

Become Need-Smart

Time for a Story

. . . .

Hole in the Bucket

Many of us know this story as a song from our childhood. It starts with Henry picking up a bucket, and singing,

> *There's a hole in the bucket, dear Liza, dear Liza,*
> *There's a hole in the bucket, dear Liza, a hole.*

See that hole in the bucket as an existential metaphor for the nature of reality. It is a little bit like the crack in everything that lets in the light in Leonard Cohen's song "Hallelujah."

Liza, who appears to have read John Gray's *Men Are from Mars, Women Are from Venus*, and knows that men think that all problems can be solved, challenges Henry with,

> *Then fix it, dear Henry, dear Henry, dear Henry,*
> *Then fix it, dear Henry, dear Henry, fix it.*

Henry looks around, and does not see anything he could use for the job. So he muses aloud:

> *With what shall I fix it, dear Liza, dear Liza?*
> *With what shall I fix it, dear Liza, with what?*

Liza keeps taunting him, and Henry keeps trying. But several verses later, it becomes apparent that to fix the bucket, water is required, and to fetch the water, a bucket is needed.

But there's a hole in the bucket . . .

Time for Reflection

. . . .

Everything everyone has ever done or will ever do,
they do to try and meet a need they have.
—MARSHALL ROSENBERG

eeds are at the center of our lives: whether we are always aware
of it or not, they drive our actions. Being mindful of our needs is
crucial, for as Rosenberg writes, "If we don't value our needs, others
may not value them either."

In our attempts to meet our needs, it is not unusual to run into a
problem with a colleague, a boss, a girlfriend, or a boyfriend. What is
our response when that happens? This is a most important question,
for our happiness and well-being do not depend on never encountering any problems in our quest for the satisfaction of our needs. They
depend on how we respond to the problems we encounter.

If we consciously focus on our need to be happy, there is a better
chance that our actions will be of the kind to bring us happiness.

Get in Touch with Your Real Needs!

In order to be need-smart, we have to know what our needs are. Unfortunately this is not always the case. We are not even always aware
of our physical needs—otherwise we would not have to go to a nutritionist, watch *The Dr. Oz Show*, or have physicians tell us that we
need to exercise. A few generations ago people did not know about
exercise—exercise pioneers were "health nuts" in those days. They
also did not know about vitamin C. We found out that we needed

that vitamin the hard way—after many people died from scurvy on long sea voyages. This is a painful way to discover needs. Do not discover your emotional needs that way. Get in touch with them by keeping an open mind and through meditation.

If many of our physical needs are a mystery, it is not surprising that our emotional needs are even more of a riddle. The late Dr. William Glasser, the originator of Reality Therapy, saw counseling as synonymous with educating clients about their basic psychological needs, and coaching them to find appropriate ways to satisfy those needs. "And how do you satisfy your need for belonging, or for fun?" his apprentice counselors were instructed to ask. If the client did not know, the counselor would then become a coach, and help the client devise appropriate strategies.

You may be intrigued to see fun listed as an essential need. But when we neglect to satisfy our need for fun, life becomes a chore or, rather, a series of chores.

Perhaps you have seen people who seem to have it all—career, money, a good marriage, children, a house . . . and yet they are not happy. Ask them what they do for fun. This may be where the problem lies. Without fun, life tends to have the taste of drudgery.

Einstein played the violin, and enjoyed getting together with other musicians to play string quartets in his spare time. He once said, "I often think in music. I daydream in music. I get most joy in life out of music." Mozart liked to play pool. He played often. There are anecdotes about him writing music while waiting for his turn at the pool table. In our day, Woody Allen enjoys playing the clarinet. He has said, "I have to practice every single day to be as bad as I am."

What do *you* do for fun?

We each satisfy our need for fun in our own way. Games for some, song and poetry, arts and crafts, movement or dance for others. Song may include Kirtan singing, choir, glee clubs, barbershop groups, song circles, or Sacred Harp groups. Arts and crafts include anything you do with your hands, including sewing, cooking, calligraphy, and gardening. Movement or dance includes T'ai Chi, yoga, acting, exercise, tennis, badminton, hockey, baseball, soccer; some forms of martial arts, such as aikido; swimming, diving, canoeing or kayaking, hiking, bicycling, and folk dancing.

Many of these are also participatory and community-building activities—you do not do folk dance or choir singing alone. As we participate in these activities, we share our energy and our enthusiasm with others. We display our talent and admire the talents of others. Most people who extol the benefits of exercise talk about its physical effects on the body. They forget that one meets new people at the gym, or on the golf course. There is a social aspect to many forms of exercise, and this can be as rewarding as its purely physical benefits. If you only exercise on a machine in your basement, you miss out on this.

It is attitude more than anything else that gives an activity the flavor of fun. It is the playful attitude. We need to find fun—enjoyment—in our hearts. Fun activities are things we choose to do because we find them intrinsically rewarding.

Notice how you feel as you lose yourself in an activity you enjoy. Do you feel fulfilled or frivolous? Rewarded or guilty?

Allow yourself to satisfy this basic need regularly.

Needs or Wants?

We usually experience our needs as "wants." The basic need may be attachment or belonging, but some of us satisfy that need by becoming a Zen monk and moving to a monastery, others by getting married, and still others by joining the Mafia. We may attempt to satisfy the same need in those different ways, but we may remain unaware of the need itself even though it is driving our behavior. But without that awareness, we may eventually behave in ways that prevent us from satisfying the need—for example, we may sabotage our marriage by having extramarital affairs. A marriage in which each person knows the value of attachment and cherishes it consciously is a deep source of happiness. It is different from one that becomes a contest of wills, and a battleground.

❖

"The wise do not hold opinions. They are aware of the needs of others," says the *Tao Te Ching*.

This is reflected elegantly in the following story:

A local Japanese girl became pregnant, and she named Hakuin, a monk in a nearby temple, as the father.

In anger the girl's father went to see Hakuin and confronted him with the accusation. "Is that so?" was all Hakuin said. The father demanded that he take care of the baby. Hakuin kindly accepted the responsibility, engaged a wet nurse, and even took the baby along on his begging rounds through the village, even though this often gave rise to scornful comments.

Sometime later the girl was overcome with guilt. She told her parents the truth—that the real father was a young man who lived nearby. The father went back to the temple in great embarrassment, and told Hakuin that he was not the father.

"Is that so?" said Hakuin once more as he returned the child.

❖

Focus on Your Needs, Not Your Emotions

Evolution primed us for responding to situations with primary feelings. Fear helps rabbits survive. Indeed, animals live by their emotions—in the absence of the highly developed cognitive ability of humans, animals' emotions serve as a kind of intelligence guiding their behavior. It makes them aware of danger signals, mate, raise their young, and respond to unexpected situations with alertness and caution.

It is surprising that "getting in touch with one's emotions" is sometimes presented as an advanced kind of accomplishment for grown women and men. But getting in touch with our *needs* is even more important. A dog or a cat feels and expresses emotions without any hesitation. Have you ever been scratched by a cat or barked at by a dog? A young child is similarly uninhibited. A baby or a toddler may not have much cognitive ability, but she can do anger or fear very well—sometimes too well—all the while not knowing what her needs are. She is only aware of her emotions. Her needs are left for the mother to guess. Is the howling child wet, hungry, sleepy, or hurting? Sometimes adults also act like that child.

In moving toward happiness and fulfillment, we need to go beyond the emotions that our needs create and focus on the needs themselves. Focusing on the emotion drives us to act out, or express that emotion. That does not necessarily fulfill the need we have. If you have been treated disrespectfully, for example, lashing out at the other person in anger will probably not satisfy your need for respect. Quite the contrary. Anger provokes anger, and you may end up getting more of the same treatment, or worse. In extreme cases, you may damage a relationship, get hurt, or even end up in jail—hardly need-fulfilling outcomes.

Move to Awareness, and to Action

An intelligent approach to our needs includes awareness of needs, but it goes beyond awareness toward smart action to satisfy them. Awareness, by itself, is not enough. Intelligence is also needed, and also flexibility and action. We can satisfy our thirst in many ways—with Coke, Pepsi, with a smoothie, spring water, or beer. The supermarket shelves are loaded with other options. What makes us choose one option over others? After perhaps fifteen years, I still remember a small girl of about five in the pueblo section of Tulum in Mexico, lovingly clutching a half-gallon bottle of Coke as she tried to carry it. The bottle looked almost as big as she was! Another story sticks in my mind: a math teacher in a small Inuit settlement in northern Manitoba told me of teenage mothers filling their babies' bottles with Pepsi. These are examples of unintelligent approaches to need fulfillment.

They are also learned responses. Soft drink aficionados learned their preference from the marketplace. But the marketplace is not a fountain of wisdom. Quite the contrary. The marketplace does not teach people to be need-smart; it teaches them unthinking brand loyalty.

Our schools are hardly better. Unless your child is attending an enlightened school, she is probably not learning to focus on and satisfy her basic needs there. She is instead mostly learning to ignore her needs, and to respond to coercion.

Emotional Paralysis

Her needs guide the life of a need-smart person. But if awareness of needs and intelligence around them are missing, then emotions take over and confuse the issue. Negative emotions are created by unsatisfied needs. One result of a lack of attention to needs is emotional blocking—sometimes called "stonewalling." I see it in people who are under pressure or emotionally abused. I see it in stressed-out women and men who are poorly treated by someone they consider important. This "important person" might be a work colleague or superior, a friend, teacher, romantic partner, or another family member. The blocked person feels that she is facing a certain disrespect or a lack of fairness, but she does not know how to respond. She is suspended between anger and fear—anger at the treatment she is getting, and fear of the consequences if she shows her anger. So, she does nothing. That creates a communication vacuum—the other person does not know about the hurt she has caused. She does not understand what is going on, and so, she keeps on acting in the same hurtful way.

Emotional blocking is what happens inside. Stonewalling is the resulting behavior.

Often the "important person" may have something significant to communicate, but she may have started on the wrong foot. When she encounters silence, she may not be sure that her point got across, so she continues, this time even more emphatically. The result? More stress, and if this is happening at work, maybe sick leave.

There is another way.

Express Your Needs

Needs are at the heart of the issue in the sort of encounters described in the aforementioned examples. They should be the focus of your message when you speak. You may need to be treated fairly and with respect, for example. If this need is not met, you may experience feelings of irritation or anger. Those feelings are a side effect that may cloud the issue. Focusing on them exclusively may get in the way of effective communication. Feelings may even get in the way of your own understanding so that you end up focusing on your anger and not on what is driving the anger—unmet needs.

The danger is that when you're focused on your emotions, this is also what you express, if not with words, then with the tone of your voice or with your body language. As a result, the person you are addressing is likely to get defensive. The discussion, which may be turning into an argument by now, gets bogged down, and your true needs are not even discussed.

Mindful Communication

Needs are about you.

Anger is directed at the other person.

Focusing on your needs keeps the focus clear. It keeps the focus on you.

Expressing our needs is not an aggressive act. It only affirms our humanity: we all have needs.

But before *expressing* needs instead of emotions such as anger, fear, or irritation, you must first *feel* those needs. You must focus on yourself instead of the other person—diagnosing, second-guessing, or pretending to read her mind. Do not go there. Stay on your side of the communication divide. Indeed, when we focus on our needs we may decide to turn the other way and run instead of communicate—if this looks like the better strategy. We may decide to change friends instead of trying to change the one we now have.

We all have some common needs:

The need to be treated with respect.
The need to be treated with kindness.
The need to be heard.
The need to sleep, rest, or take a break.

When a need is frustrated, a whole gamut of emotions can be felt. These emotions have a purpose: to signal unmet needs. Notice them and observe them, but do not act them out. Do not behave "emotionally," in the negative sense of the word. Emotions can be discussed without being "emotional." But in order to succeed in this, we must go beyond the emotions to the needs they are pointing at. An emotion such as fear, for example, arises to signal to us that our need for safety is not being met. That is the role of emotion. Once we have connected with the need for safety, fear has already done its job. When the time comes to communicate with others, it can get in the way. Two people yelling at each other are being emotional in the negative sense of the word—two people peacefully discussing their needs are more likely to come to an understanding. They may be emotional in the positive sense of the word—they may be aware of their emotions, without acting them out.

If the other person is being emotional, focus on their need. If the need is not clear, ask—if there is a problem, that is where it is. The emotions are just the froth on the surface. You may find that the person you are facing is not clear about her needs. If that is the case, that discussion is not going to have a solution. Try to get out of the way without getting hurt.

If you are the one who is overwhelmed by emotions, keep asking yourself what your needs are. Another way to do this is to ask yourself what would make you happy.

Set Your Compass to Your Needs

Needs are basic. When our psychological needs are consistently denied, we may go into a tailspin, show symptoms of depression or anxiety, or get close to a nervous breakdown. Compare this with physical needs: if our need for water, air, or food is consistently denied, we wilt.

Dr. William Glasser, with whom I had the privilege of studying, made a thorough examination of the distinction between needs and wants. Here is an example that will make the difference clear: We all need food. But when we are hungry, some of us want a hamburger, some a soup, and some a salad. Our needs are felt through our preferences. Those preferences are our wants. We feel and express our needs through our wants. But our wants are often shaped by our habits, and strangely enough, they do not always satisfy the need. Example: We are thirsty, and our habit pushes us to have a sugary soda. But the sugar-laden drink makes us even thirstier: when sugar enters the bloodstream and begins to circulate through the body, it draws water from all the cells in the body. Your body then sends out chemical messages to the brain to say that it's time to drink more fluids. Then, if you drink more soda, the whole cycle starts over without satisfying your thirst. Soft-drink makers are happy. Your body isn't.

There is a need behind a want. Getting in touch with that need will make it possible to be flexible and effective in satisfying the need. This understanding, though not always clearly articulated, is what drives numerous episodes of *The Dr. Oz Show*. Dr. Mehmet Oz does not recommend that overweight people stop eating. Instead, he recommends satisfying the need for food in different, healthier ways. Food is a *need*. We cannot change that. But we can change what we *want* to eat. We can eat green vegetables instead of French fries, for example, and protein and fiber-rich beans instead of carbohydrate-rich pasta.

French fries are not a need; they are a want, even though a child who is brought up on them may not agree. *Food* is the need. The transition from fries to healthier items may not be possible without getting in touch with the need behind the want, and changing our focus from the want to the need.

A craving for comfort foods may be driven by needs other than food. Say that you feel like having ice cream. Ask yourself if it is really ice cream you need, or do you just need a treat, maybe some fun? When you get in touch with the need, it becomes possible to make substitutions: maybe you can have tea or coffee instead, or an apple. Perhaps you can call a friend and chat with her for a bit, or go for a short walk in the sun. Such substitutions would only be possible if the need was clear.

A similar approach also works for psychological needs such as love. It is love that we all need, rather than the love of a particular person. Stalkers are not aware of the difference between needs and wants, and get fixated on a certain individual who does not want to have anything to do with them. Many stalkers end up harming the person they "love."

The Scottish folk song "Wild Mountain Thyme" describes a refreshingly different attitude:

> *Oh, the summer time has come*
> *And the trees are sweetly bloomin'*
> *And the wild mountain thyme*
> *Grows around the bloomin' heather*
> *Will ye go, lassie, go?*
>
> *And we'll all go together*
> *To pull wild mountain thyme*
> *All around the bloomin' heather*
> *Will ye go, lassie, go?*
>
> *If my true love she'll not come*
> *Then I'll surely find another*
> *To pull wild mountain thyme*
> *All around the bloomin' heather*
> *Will ye go, lassie, go?*

When I first heard that song, I disliked the beginning of the last verse, because I imagined the lover saying it to his love. I found it a very unromantic way to romance someone. But no, there the voice has changed from "ye" to "she." He's saying that to himself: he's musing. Then, he turns back to her once more, and repeats his request. He is not fixated, only persistent.

This young man's attitude toward love also applies to careers. Many people change careers easily. Their attitude toward meaningful work is similar to the lover's in this song: if they are not happy in one career or job, they feel that they will "surely find another." A positive state of mind and a heart full of confidence make this easier. My partner and I have both changed careers more than once. The U.S. average is five to seven career changes during a lifetime.

Let us keep in mind that our goal is happiness, not necessarily happiness with a particular person or in a particular job. Meaningful work and meaningful relationships are *needs*. Success in a particular job or the love of a particular person are *wants*. As we change our focus from wants to needs, we are more likely to be flexible and succeed in finding happiness.

Controlling Behavior—A Red Flag!

Controlling behavior can be quite unconscious or even well-meaning. We ourselves act a certain way, drive, wash dishes, and even eat a certain way because we think that's the right way to do it. Be aware of your inner backseat driver. She may be getting on someone's nerves. No one likes to be someone else's puppet. Recognize controlling behavior in yourself and in others. It can range anywhere from urging someone to have another drink to belittling them for what they do or what they are. It can easily slip into a power trip. "Instead of controlling things, the sage ceases to be obstructed by them," writes A. C. Graham in *The Book of Lieh-Tzu*. This applies to trying to control the behavior of teenagers as well as of other drivers on the road.

Much has already been written about controlling behavior—

someone else's controlling behavior, as if only other people do it. Also, it takes two to tango, and we may be complying implicitly with the controller. Mindfulness helps us to recognize this, and not get caught up in it.

❊

Ich Habe Genug

"There is no greater curse than discontent. If you know that enough is enough, you will always have enough," says the *Tao Te Ching*.

"I have enough" or "I am content" in its English translation, *Ich Habe Genug* is the most often performed and the most often recorded of J. S. Bach's two hundred or so cantatas. The words refer to the contentment that comes from spiritual fulfillment. There are many versions of this lovely cantata on YouTube; you can listen to it as a tool for the practice of contentment—the music reflects the words faithfully.

The third movement of the cantata adds a related theme—the connection between contentment and the ability to let go and fall asleep: "Fall asleep, you weary eyes, close softly and pleasantly!" The sleep in question here is death, the ultimate sleep. Statistics say that 68 percent of us have death-related anxiety. This is roughly the same percentage as the people who have sleep difficulties. Perhaps the real issue is the difficulty of giving up a sense of control, and of letting go with the contented feeling of having had a rich and full day, or a rich and full life.

A Thich Nhat Hanh calligraphy that echoes Bach says, "You Have Enough." This calligraphy is unusual in that the text is written in English as well as in Chinese characters, pointing out the source of Thich Nhat Hanh's inspiration in Chinese Buddhism. This is a wonderful convergence of the two spiritual paths of Christianity and Buddhism.

However, there is one path that strongly diverges from the cultivation of contentment, and that is our contemporary culture. Dissatisfaction with what we have and what we look like is promoted daily and hourly by the media. The demand for plastic surgery is at an all-time high, and we are constantly urged to buy more things. This gives us another reason to cultivate contentment in our meditation practice, because we need to counteract the daily indoctrination that the media serves us. Without mindfulness, we can easily succumb to the media barrage, and end up being convinced that buying more things will make us happier.

Contentment comes from appreciating what we have.

Discontent comes from dwelling on what we lack—what we do not have.

To increase contentment, we do not necessarily have to get more things—we just have to appreciate what we already have.

When discontent arises, shift your focus from what you lack toward what you have.

Time for Practice

. . . .

Meditation Theme: Meditation on Resilience

I'm sitting on a hill above the banks of the Saint Lawrence River, watching the oak leaves dancing in the light breeze.

The leaves tug at the branches like the sail tugs at the sailboat, making them bend and bow with the wind.

The branches flex and warp in every direction, then come back again.

Again and again, sometimes for days and nights on end.

Through all this, the tree keeps its stately shape, not because it encounters no challenges, but because every part of it is resilient.

The deer in the mountains go through cold winters where it snows on their fur.

Sometimes there is no food for days and weeks.

No leaves in sight, and grasses are covered with snow.

Pregnancy, birth, and child-rearing are all done in the open, under the rain.

They live and thrive, not because there are no trials and difficulties in the wild, but because they are resilient.

Resilience is built into nature. We all have it.

In difficult times remember this, and reach for that resource that is within you.

Resilience bends, but springs back again and again—it is flexible.

The deer do not fight with the seasons—they adapt to them.
The oak leaves do not fight the wind—they dance to it.

Visualize the deer in the mountains, on a cold night without
food.
They have needs, but not expectations. They accept what comes.
They watch as night turns to day, and winter turns to spring.

Take a few deep breaths.
Stay with the sensations of breathing.
Get in touch with your needs.
Observe your expectations. Know the difference.
Smile.
Come back to your focus on the breath.
It's the body that breathes.
Let the mind join the body in breathing.
Let the mind also breathe.

Practice Song: First, Find the Beauty in Your Own Heart

First, find the beauty in your own heart
And then sing a song, or take a walk,
You'll see flowers bloom all around.
Find the beauty, in your own heart
You'll see flowers bloom all around.

The most basic way of practicing with this song is visualizing the beauty of nature as you sit—the beauty of a moonlit night, of a flowering meadow, or of a child. You have also been that child. That beauty of a child is still there in you if you look deeply. Bask in the beauty of nature—your own nature—as you sit. Practicing with this theme will make beauty a reality in your life.

Beauty does not have to be skin deep. The English poet John Keats wrote:

> *Beauty is truth, truth beauty—that is all*
> *ye know on earth, and all ye need to know.*

Participants in a group came up with some other appropriate ways for practicing with this song that I had not thought of before. One martial arts practitioner spoke of the importance of finding peace and beauty in his heart before sparring with a partner. Otherwise the dynamics of face-to-face training can give rise to hard feelings or even injury. Another, a school bus driver, mentioned the importance of first finding peace in himself in the morning before starting his rounds. Kids can be trying at times! This brought smiles of recognition from the commuters as well as the parents in the group. Many drivers of all kinds get on the road with impatience and aggressiveness in their hearts instead of peace and beauty.

You may not be in touch with your own beauty. If so, this song will connect you with it. Practicing with this theme, practicing walking with beauty, speaking with beauty, and doing everyday things with beauty brings it closer to the surface so that the beauty of your true nature can shine forth every moment. For others, our innate beauty may not be far from our awareness. Then this song is a gentle reminder.

Chapter 7

Embrace Work,
Embrace "Laziness"

Time for a Story

Touring China with Thich Nhat Hanh
(A Personal Story)

Thich Nhat Hanh was preparing to go to China. The trip was to be a combination of a teaching tour and a pilgrimage—he was slated to visit and give talks in ancient monasteries that I only knew about from stories. When I heard that his lay students could join the trip, I jumped at the chance—together with about three hundred others.

Soon after I signed up, I received the schedule and had second thoughts. Each hour of the day was filled with activities such as temple visits, talks, and travel. It seemed pretty exhausting. I went to Sister Annabel Laity, who was one of the organizers, and mentioned my misgivings: "There does not seem to be any time for rest," I said.

"Why don't you rest while you are participating in the activities?" she suggested.

I had not considered that possibility.

Time for Reflection

. . . .

In every cry of every Man,
In every Infant's cry of fear,
In every voice, in every ban,
The mind-forg'd manacles I hear.
—WILLIAM BLAKE

In the sometimes-puzzling language of Zen, laziness means a break from *doing*.

It does not mean a break from *being*—being concentrated, being peaceful, or being compassionate.

One can be very busy without being concentrated, peaceful, or compassionate—or without being oneself. Stress is made worse by this kind of busyness.

We go to university willingly even though it is stressful to study for exams and write term papers. Some of us choose to run marathons, even though it is one of the most stressful things I can think of—there were a couple of deaths at this year's Montreal Marathon. Volunteer doctors join Doctors Without Borders and put their lives at risk out of choice. Even working out at the gym involves stress—we stress our body willingly in order to keep it in shape.

Leading a life of meaning and working for something we believe in is one of the most compelling components of happiness for many of us, even though it usually involves some stress as well. But notice a couple of things about this kind of voluntary stress.

First, it is chosen—we can also choose to stop it if we want to.

This means that we are not conflicted about it. No one is pushing us, and we are not doing things out of a sense of duty or obligation. We are one with our goals, values, and actions. That infuses what we do with enthusiasm and serenity, for it is mental conflict that eats up energy.

Second, voluntary stress is usually intermittent—we are not running marathons or working out at the gym 24/7. University life also includes recreation, fun activities, and parties. The kind of stress that grinds us down and makes us sick is unrelenting stress. Without mindfulness, the mind can go 24/7 even though the body is desperately trying to rest, or even to sleep. Unrelenting stress exhausts the adrenal glands, with the result being that we eventually feel worn out. As I made clear in my book *Buddha's Book of Stress Reduction*, problems arise when the mind keeps going even when the body stops. The mind does not always know how to stop. But true rest is not possible unless the mind is at rest. Body and mind are one, and a restless mind gives no respite to the body.

Stress Reduction Through Personal Growth

Mindfulness-based personal growth fosters self-knowledge and self-understanding. Contrast this with the title of a well-known book on mental illness: *Strangers to Themselves*. Becoming more intimate with oneself is a healing practice, not only for people who have slid into mental illness, but for all of us. It involves becoming aware of the fact that energies such as compulsive work habits and anger are inside us. They drive us from the inside. As we recognize that, our notion of "self" undergoes subtle changes. We stop identifying with every voice that comes from our brain. We are not only a bundle of habits. We are also the one who carries that bundle on her back. That realization is healing, for the one who carries the bundle can always put it down.

I own a Tibetan *thangka* that looks like a geometrical maze. *Thangka*s are Tibetan paintings usually depicting traditional deities, and they help us to visualize the energies they represent. At the very

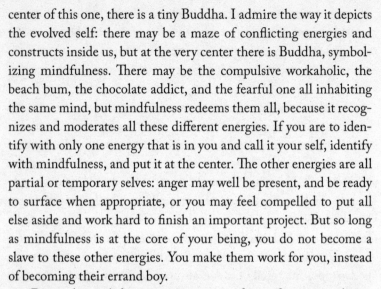

center of this one, there is a tiny Buddha. I admire the way it depicts the evolved self: there may be a maze of conflicting energies and constructs inside us, but at the very center there is Buddha, symbolizing mindfulness. There may be the compulsive workaholic, the beach bum, the chocolate addict, and the fearful one all inhabiting the same mind, but mindfulness redeems them all, because it recognizes and moderates all these different energies. If you are to identify with only one energy that is in you and call it your self, identify with mindfulness, and put it at the center. The other energies are all partial or temporary selves: anger may well be present, and be ready to surface when appropriate, or you may feel compelled to put all else aside and work hard to finish an important project. But so long as mindfulness is at the core of your being, you do not become a slave to these other energies. You make them work for you, instead of becoming their errand boy.

Personal growth does not mean negating facets of our personality—that would make for a pretty bland kind of person. It means gaining the freedom to be your true self, still owning the full palette of colors inside but not becoming compulsively monochromatic. Considering a part of the self as the whole—or treating a temporary self as a permanent one—is a distortion, and creates its own measure of stress.

I see stress reduction and personal growth as two sides of the same coin. Without a mental change, physical change is not effective. City folk who move to the country often take their stress along with them—they do not leave it behind. Embrace stress, but do not become a stress junkie. Know your limits. Take time to enjoy life. The word "workaholic" expresses a mindless attitude to work. That attitude may have been fostered by our upbringing. Our parents and teachers constantly exhorted us to get off the couch and do homework. They created demanding schedules of recreation, music lessons, and often housework as well. Many of us have ended up internalizing their voices.

Laziness—Sin or Virtue?

Laziness is one of the seven deadly sins of Catholicism, and it is also viewed negatively in other traditions, including Buddhism. But let's look a little closer.

At the Jewish General Hospital, one of the large university hospitals in Montreal, the elevators are programmed to stop on every floor on Saturdays. That is because if you are Jewish, you are not supposed to do anything that feels like work on the Sabbath, and even pushing an elevator button is considered "work." Observing the Sabbath is a sort of mindful laziness.

A similar current runs through Catholicism. When I was younger, all the stores—including grocery stores—were closed on Sundays in Québec, a largely Catholic part of Canada. Sunday was the Lord's Day. Even mowing the lawn on Sunday was looked down upon.

Thich Nhat Hanh has adopted a similar tradition at Plum Village in France. I was with Helen, a friend, when she called Plum Village to make a reservation for a retreat. There were cascades of laughter at the other end of the line. "We are having a lazy day today, please call back tomorrow" was the short answer Helen got before the line went silent. Indeed, Thich Nhat Hanh is not shy about describing himself as a "lazy monk."

Finding Balance

In answering a question, Thich Nhat Hanh once said, "In our society, we're inclined to see doing nothing as something negative, even evil. But when we lose ourselves in activities we diminish our quality of being. We do ourselves a disservice. It's important to preserve ourselves, to maintain our freshness and good humor, our joy and compassion."

He himself has been a hard worker, but his work has been an expression of his being. His work is of the kind I describe at the beginning of this chapter—it is undertaken out of choice, not obligation. And it is relieved by periods of rest and relaxation. Many years ago, I met an elderly Vietnamese monk who had been Thich Nhat Hanh's roommate while he was working on *Old Path White Clouds: Walking in the Footsteps of the Buddha*. He described a fluent and nonstop clatter of the typewriter day after day. However, Thich Nhat Hanh also recounts times from his novice days when he used to sneak away to a tree house he had constructed and read a novel. When he sometimes sounds as if he is promoting laziness, he is actually promoting a balanced life, because he knows that the "work/rest" balance has been largely lost in our society.

Practicing "Laziness"

Just like there is a place for voluntary stress, there is a place for voluntary laziness in a happy life. People who are "constitutionally" happy instinctively make room for both. The rest of us need to learn to do this if we are not going to join the legions who suffer from exhaustion and burnout. Voluntary laziness is not procrastination. It is not an *inability* to get to work. It is an *ability* to take a break. Meditation can help us to enjoy the calm inside, and to listen to the silence of the mind.

"The basic condition for us to be able to hear the call of beauty and respond to it is silence. If we don't have silence in ourselves—if our mind, our body, are full of noise—then we can't hear beauty's call," writes Thich Nhat Hanh. Beauty is everywhere around us, in the smiles of people, in the fragrance and colors of flowers, in the blue sky and in the white clouds that sail across it. Sometimes people describe to me the difficulty of maintaining a blank state of mind in meditation. That seems to me like a negatively conceived effort. Instead, fill your heart and mind with beauty. Visualize a flower. Visualize that flower in your heart. Visualize a whole garden in your heart, blooming with roses of love, irises of gratitude, and dandelions of freshness. Enjoy your garden, just like you would enjoy an actual flowering garden.

There are more suggestions for your daily meditation practice in the Time for Practice section at the end of the chapter.

Restlessness

Hamsters are always running in their wheels. Squirrels are jumping from branch to branch. When my daughters were young, we made an attempt to have rabbits as house pets. We managed to toilet train them, but we could not overcome their need to snack on furniture. We still have some furniture with nibbled-on legs from those days. Those rabbits were well fed and cared for. They did not have to chew on treated wood, but they just could not stop that habit energy.

We humans are a bit like that in some ways as well. We have the habit of putting something in front of us and running after it. That something can be a ball, a puck, or climbing a mountain. While there's nothing intrinsically bad about those things, doing them compulsively takes away much of the pleasure. There's nothing playful about professional hockey or baseball, and nothing recreational about climbing Mount Everest.

I was present at a retreat when Thich Nhat Hanh was asked what he thought Israelis and Palestinians should do in order to have peace. "Nothing," he replied. "If they do nothing, there will be peace."

There are over two hundred corpses on Mount Everest. Many people die every day because of reckless driving. How can such deaths be prevented? I can almost hear Thich Nhat Hanh saying, "If these people can enjoy doing nothing, they will not die like that."

Thich Nhat Hanh is suggesting that we become aware of our restlessness. Restlessness can lead us by the nose, but only if we are not mindful of it.

Time-Related Stress

Many people say that time is their principal cause of stress. They are working hard to beat the clock. There is a better way. It is to come to a better understanding of time, and of what makes the clock tick.

Time is embodied. That is the short message I get from all the dizzying equations that make up the theory of relativity.

It makes no sense to think of it as an abstract entity.

It makes no sense to think of it as existing apart, separate from all the stuff of the universe, keeping an eye on electrons and on planets, making sure that their rotations stick to a prearranged schedule.

It is rather the other way around: those rotations define time, and are what we measure time with.

"Time goes; the clocks barely keep up," writes Wendell Berry. Our steps, our breath, our life measure time.

Remember that the next time you feel time pressure or time-related stress.

Only One Thing at a Time

You never have ten things to do. You only have one thing to do. Always. Because you can only do one thing at a time.

Do it well. Enjoy your time with it. Then, give yourself a reward for a job well done—anything from a cup of coffee to just a smile.

Now, again, you only have one thing to do: the next thing.

Soon, you will be able to look back on a productive day.

The rosebush does not get stressed thinking that it has to bloom on the twenty-second of May. It measures time with days of sunshine and buckets of rain, and not by the distant church bells it hears. The bloom will be done when it is time. This does not mean that the rosebush is idle. It is constantly at work, getting ready for B-day. Just because you do not see it looking busy, do not jump to conclusions. It is busy enjoying the sun, enjoying the rain, and enjoying the bees that come for a visit. That is how it works.

"Patience joins time to eternity," writes Wendell Berry. Time-related stress is often coupled with impatience. Trying to "beat the clock" is doomed to failure and to result in stress. Clocks are hard to beat, because they measure abstract time. But we have bodies. We are on embodied time. This creates a basic conflict between them and us. Yes, buses, trains, and work all have schedules. Thich Nhat Hanh's advice? Cooperate with those schedules instead of fighting with them. Instead of doing three things before you leave home, do just one. Do it well. Enjoy your time doing it. That way you are not in a rush to be on time for the bus or the train.

You do not have to be a poet only when you are writing a poem. You can be a poet all the time if you live with mindfulness.

Again quoting Wendell Berry: "There are no unsacred places; there are only sacred places and desecrated places." There is nothing quite like always being in a rush to make me feel desecrated.

Tune Your Guitar

In a collection of Buddha's discourses known as the *Anguttara Nikaya*, there is a conversation with Sona, a stringed instrument player. Let us add a contemporary touch, and picture that stringed instrument as a guitar, and Sona as a guitar player. In the story, Sona wants to improve his meditation skills, practices very hard, does not get the results he wants as quickly as he would like, and is frustrated. He is on the verge of quitting. Here is a detail that gives an idea of Sona's excess of zeal: he practiced walking meditation so intensively that his feet were bleeding.

Buddha, ever ready to put his teachings in a context that would make sense to his interlocutors, talks to him about tuning the guitar: in order to produce good music, the strings need to be just the right tightness—not too slack, not too tight. It is the same with mindfulness practice. Practiced with the wrong attitude, meditation itself can become a source of stress rather than an antidote to it.

Buddha ends the conversation with, "In the same way, Sona, over-aroused persistence leads to restlessness, overly slack persistence leads to laziness. You have been straining too hard in your meditation. Do it in a relaxed way, but without being slack. Determine the right pitch for your persistence." Sona follows Buddha's advice, and succeeds in finding the "right pitch." Soon, he is able to meditate with a mind that is "neither overpowered nor even engaged" by thoughts. Even when powerful thoughts come within the range of his mind, he is able to just watch them as they pass away.

Perceived Stress vs. Objective Measures of Stress

These days, I experience less physical stress lifting a hundred-pound barbell than I did when I was a beginner and only lifting fifty pounds. And there are plenty of people at the gym who lift heavier weights with ease. Conclusion: the subjective feeling of stress is not necessarily proportional to the task at hand. It varies with training, and also from person to person.

Objective measures of stress exist. One of them is measuring the level of cortisol (the stress hormone) in the saliva. According to research, it is a reliable predictor of being at risk for heart disease. Yet, it is important to realize that this *objective* test is only a measure of *subjective* levels of stress, for stress is not always proportional to responsibilities or to hours at work. What is even more daunting is that "subjective" does not always mean "felt." Many people are under stress without being aware of it. A heart attack comes out of the blue for them.

"Defeating" Stress

In doing research for this book, I came upon an article in the *Harvard Business Review* with the title "Nine Ways Successful People Defeat Stress." The title raised my hackles: not all successful people defeat stress. *Happy* people defeat stress. Many others, including some successful people, are defeated by stress. Happiness is the focus of my book. Success is the focus of the *HBR*. In real life sometimes the receptionist is happier than the president of the corporation. The article uses military metaphors such as *defeat* in the title and *strategies* in the introduction. Again this is consistent with the competitive bias of its readers. Nevertheless, I agree with its premise that dealing successfully with stress is a learnable skill. It is an essential skill for happiness. Still, I think that "tuning a guitar string" is a better metaphor for this than "defeat"—for lack of stress does not necessarily make you happy. We *crave* some amount of stress—the right amount.

Happy people seem to have a knack for judging that, and keeping their stress within bounds.

Where do they learn how to tune the strings of their hearts to the right pitch? There is a story about Mozart, one of the most astounding child prodigies ever. At a very young age his father took him to a music teacher for instruction. Whenever the teacher tried to teach him something, the young Mozart would say, "Yes, of course. I know all that." Was he born knowing? In his case there was a happy coincidence, and genes and upbringing converged—he was born into a musical family. Johann Georg Leopold Mozart, his father, was a well-known composer, conductor, teacher, and violinist in his own right. Perhaps his son was able to simply absorb the musical language in which he was immersed, like we all absorb the language of our parents.

In the school of happiness, some of us are child prodigies like Mozart, and some slow learners.

However, there is a key difference between learning to play the piano and learning happiness skills: you can live very well without playing the piano. You can live without happiness, but not very well.

Time for Practice

Guided Meditation: Being on the Edge of Time

❖

*Take a few moments to get in touch with your breath, and slow
  it down.*
Right now, are you in this moment, or in the next moment?
If you are in the next moment,
    what makes you get ahead of yourself?
Is it impatience, restlessness, boredom, or anxiety?
Discover what drives it. Is this a habit you have?
If you are in the next moment, it is the mind that goes there.
The body is still here.
Gently bring the body and mind together.
Bring the mind to focus on the senses.

❖

If, instead, you are in a past moment,
    what makes you get stuck there?
Let it go, whatever it is, and come back to your body now.
Come back to your breath and to your senses.
You have already lived that previous moment;
    it has a familiar feel.
Let it go. Come back to this breath, the one you are taking now.

❖

This moment is uncertain, and fresh.
Being in the moment feels like being on the edge—
    on the edge of time.
Practice staying here,
    with this breath and this moment's sensations.
Going to the past or the future can be a form of daydreaming.
If thoughts about the past or the future are accompanied by
emotions, you may be daydreaming.

❖

You can contemplate the past or the future
    without getting lost in the past or the future.
Consider that the past is just memory,
    and the future is imagination.
Remind yourself of this often.
Memory and imagination are not our enemies.
They can also be our friends. The question is,
    "Who is in charge?"

Practice Song: It's Time for a Break

It's time for a break:
Breathe in, breathe out,
This is your home, the only home you have known,
You and the sun, you and the clouds
Have come to be together many moons ago.

Find peace where you are,
Be at ease in your heart,
Enjoy your day.

The important thing about a break is not so much the length, but the quality of it.

In this song, the break is seen as an opportunity to come back to a relaxed, natural state of being, a state like that of a soaring seagull or of grasses swaying in the wind.

It is to momentarily switch off from a state of doing to a state of being. It is coming out of the pressure cooker and mentally lying on a hammock. And then going back to work in that relaxed state of mind. Once you get there, hang on to that relaxed state as long as you can, if possible for the rest of the day.

The third line is in effect saying, "Make yourself at home." For we are at home here on Earth.

Chapter 8

Grow Through Meditation

Time for a Story

. . . .

What Is the Purpose?

A student who had been meditating by himself for a long time went to see a Zen master. He wanted to make sure that he was practicing correctly.

The master asked him, "What is the purpose?"

The student had no answer. He went home to think about it.

Soon, he came back, and the master asked the same question. The meditator still did not know how to answer, but now he had a question:

"Is there a purpose?"

"I mean, how is your practice used?" asked the master.

Another few days, and the meditator was back again. He had decided to turn the tables and ask the master his own question.

"How is it used?"

Just then, a sparrow started singing in the yard.

"You hear the sparrow when it sings," said the master.

Time for Reflection

....

To be beautiful means to be yourself.
You don't need to be accepted by others. You need to
accept yourself.
—THICH NHAT HANH

What is the best way to meditate? Should your mind be empty while you sit? Can you think while sitting in meditation?

These are important questions, and your attitude toward them has much to do with how effective your meditation practice is going to be. Here is what some meditation teachers have said on these subjects, and my comments:

1. In *The Book of Equanimity*, Gerry Shishin Wick writes, "There is a notion among Zen students that they should not use their reasoning faculties when practicing meditation." He avows that he also had that notion when he was a beginner. He continues with, "I believe thinking in meditative disciplines has been given a bum rap."

Beware of labeling all mental activity as "thinking." Inspiration, insight, awakening, and enlightenment are all activities of the mind, and they are much prized among meditators. What is the difference between these and "thinking," which is often put down? To what extent can we separate them?

This question came up when I asked Lena for feedback after a meditation period. She started every sentence with, "I was think-

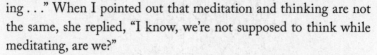

ing . . ." When I pointed out that meditation and thinking are not the same, she replied, "I know, we're not supposed to think while meditating, are we?"

Well, there is thinking, and thinking . . . Buddha had his insight while meditating. Was he thinking? Insight (Kensho) is also at the heart of Zen practice, and the primary Buddhist mode of meditation is called Insight Meditation (Vipassana). However, I cannot imagine it being referred to as "Thinking Meditation"! The distinction between thinking and insight is important, and not only during the meditation period. Here are some examples that may make it clear.

Sir Isaac Newton is credited with coming up with the theory of gravity after he saw an apple fall from a tree. The falling of the apple was a momentary event, but much training in mathematics and physics must have gone into preparing Newton's mind for that insight. I assume that the formal statement of the theory of universal gravitation also included equations and a proof, all of which required thinking. But the insight itself was sudden. The version I was originally taught as a schoolboy dramatized the instantaneous nature of it by saying that the apple had actually fallen on his head.

Insight is an intense momentary experience. It is the eureka moment. The accumulated observations and experiences of a lifetime may go into it, but it bursts into our awareness in an instant. Buddha meditated for six years, but his awakening is described as having occurred on a particular moment before dawn on a certain day.

The moment of giving birth is another metaphor for insight. The gestation period is out of sight (in the sense that we do not see what is actually going on inside the womb), and out of mind (in the sense that a pregnant woman is not growing the fetus consciously). During birth, all that background activity bursts into the light of day as a complete baby. In a similar way, insights can gestate in the mind before breaking into awareness. We can be thinking unconsciously. Thinking and insight are related: so far, no one has come up with a way to have a baby without going through nine months of pregnancy.

Still, beware of the Pied Piper effect. According to a medieval German legend, the town of Hamelin was once infested with rats, and all efforts to get rid of them had failed. Then, this colorful, brightly dressed character showed up, and offered to do the job. He played an irresistible tune on his pipe that lured all the town's rats to come out of their holes and follow him. He then led them down to the river, where they all drowned.

In the legend, this same Pied Piper also has a malicious side: he returns, and this time lures all the town's children away.

Thinking can be like that Pied Piper. We tend to follow our thoughts whether we want to or not—sometimes this makes us happy, and sometimes unhappy.

Thinking does not necessarily lead to insight—we can get lost in thought, following a thought here, and another one there, and just getting more and more distracted. Thought is often a train with many wagons—we follow a *train* of thought. It may lead to heaven or to hell; make sure you read the destination sign above the driver's window before embarking.

One more thing: moments of insight are not necessarily verbal. Often they are visceral, like a gut feeling. Coming to one's senses itself is a kind of awakening—it is an awakening from going round and round in one's thoughts, and getting deeper and deeper into a verbal vortex. The light is not at the bottom of a well, but up above where the sun is shining.

2. In his book *The Art of Happiness at Work*, cowritten with the Dalai Lama, Howard Cutler writes that some meditators try to become "thoughtless, freer of thoughts" during their practice. He compares that kind of meditation to "going on a picnic or taking a painkiller." He continues, "Some people may spend years doing these practices, but their actual progress is zero."

The ability to empty the mind when it is filled with negativity or with trivial things is part of the practice. But that is not the ultimate goal. I do empty my mind when I start to sit. Then I breathe, and wait. It is like a patch of ground I would clear of weeds to make a garden. I do not do that just so that I have an empty plot for a garden. Soon, little flowers begin to come out of the ground. Those flowers are what you are reading now. They are also the songs and practices I hope you are using as you go through this book.

Empty your mind of preconceptions and certainties. They limit your vision to what you already know. Each moment presents us with a unique situation, one that has not yet occurred in the history of the world. There is something in this moment that does not fit any historical blueprint. Ideally, learning and experience show us *how* past problems were solved. They serve as examples—they are not there to limit us to those past solutions.

There is a story about an empty versus a full mind. Once, a university professor was visiting a Zen master. He wanted to learn about Zen. The master invited him to have a cup of tea with him. He started pouring tea into the professor's cup. The cup was soon full. The master continued to pour. Soon there was tea all over the saucer, and some was going on the table.

"Stop!" the professor exclaimed. "Don't you see that the cup is full?"

"Your mind is like this cup," said the master. "It is already full. How can I teach you Zen if your mind is already full?"

But did that Zen master himself have an empty mind? Empty of what? Even if we agree that an empty mind is a good thing for a Zen master, would it be a good thing for a university professor? How would an empty-minded professor teach his classes? These questions go to the heart of the matter.

Consider the coffee cup on the table. It gets full and empty many times a day. In between, it gets full of dishwater. Do you want that cup full of dishwater? The barista does not want it either. She wants an empty cup, just like the Zen master. And I want a cup of fresh coffee, this moment's coffee, not yesterday's stale coffee.

An "empty" cup is not really empty anyway—it is full of air. We live on the Earth, and our environment is full of air. Air itself consists of a number of different gases, including some car exhaust, humidity, and human breath. We do not entirely control what is in our cup. Our cup reflects our environment to some extent. Mindfulness is the ability to experience the cup, and not just be mesmerized by its contents.

Do not stop with the mind, though. Also empty the basement, the fridge, and the kitchen cupboard from time to time. Just like the mind, those places are also most useful when there is some space in them. The interplay between form and usefulness was pointed out most eloquently in the *Tao Te Ching* (#11):

> *There are many spokes in a carriage wheel,*
> *But it is the hole in the center that makes it useful.*
> *The cup is made of glass,*
> *But it is the empty space inside that makes it useful.*
> *Doors and windows are made from all kinds of*
> *   materials,*
> *But it is the empty opening that makes them useful.*
> *What there is gives a thing its form,*
> *But it is what is not there that makes it useful.*

This interplay also applies to meditation. A mind that is full of negativity or of set notions is not open to change, new discoveries, or growth.

3. **"My teaching is a means of practice, not something to hold onto or worship. My teaching is like a raft used to cross the river. Only a fool would carry the raft around after he had already reached the other shore, the shore of liberation," writes Thich Nhat Hanh in *Old Path White Clouds*.**

In this text, Thich Nhat Hanh is summarizing a passage in a talk the Buddha once gave. The talk has been preserved as the *Alagaddupama Sutta*. Here is a free translation of the appropriate section from this discourse: "Suppose a man were walking along a path and he saw a great expanse of water that he needed to cross, but with neither a ferryboat nor a bridge going from this shore to the other. He notices a number of large logs and pieces of rope lying about. He decides to put together a makeshift raft with them, and manages to paddle across with it. Once on the other shore, he realizes how precious and helpful this raft has been to him, and doesn't want to let it go. He says to himself, 'Why don't I just hoist it on my head or carry it on my back wherever I go?'"

Perhaps you know someone who is carrying spiritual teachings around on his back wherever he goes? The problem is that the teachings are on his back—they are not part of him. They are separate from him. This is a tricky teaching nevertheless! We cross that expanse of water Buddha talks about in this text not just once in a lifetime, but at every turn. I do not blame that man for wanting to hang on to his raft.

Meditation is a *means* toward growth and a happier life.

Do not put it on a pedestal and worship it.

Put *life* on a pedestal instead.

Once it is assimilated, the practice becomes part of us, and weighs nothing. It is more like learning to swim than carrying a heavy wooden raft. Mindfulness fundamentals such as "Being in the moment," "Focusing on the breath," and "Doing one thing at a time" need to be applied to our life in order to be useful. They are not injunctions to be observed for their own sake.

Keeping this in mind has two important consequences: it motivates us to practice mindfulness for the right reasons and it stimulates us to apply our meditation practice to practical issues. "The devil is in the details," as the saying goes. Not only the devil, but mindfulness is also in the details.

True Growth

Loud. Self-centered. Inconsiderate. Easily upset.

Those descriptions applied to all of us once—we have all been babies and toddlers. But we improved through growth.

Meditation fosters lifelong growth.

Fresh. Spontaneous. In the moment. Joyful.

Those descriptions also applied to us as young children.

Paradoxically, as we grow through mindfulness meditation, we keep those precious qualities of childhood.

Some Dos and One Don't

1. MEDITATE—DO NOT RUMINATE

Meditation is like grazing; rumination is like burping what was previously chewed and swallowed. Indeed, with grazing animals it is exactly that. To continue the metaphor, in meditation there is choice. The grazing animal chooses what it puts into its mouth—maybe some sweet clover or delicious-smelling mint. In rumination the animal just chews over what comes up, thorns and all.

Thich Nhat Hanh's verse "Waking Up This Morning" is an example of a morning meditation:

> *Waking up this morning, I see the blue sky,*
> *I join my hands in thankfulness for the many*
> *wonders of life.*

In contrast, a period of morning rumination may go as follows:

> *Waking up this morning, I think of yesterday's missed*
> *opportunities*
> *And consider everything that may go wrong today.*

Rumination brings stress. Meditation brings relief, for it enlarges perspective and context.

An inexperienced meditator is easily caught in rumination, especially if she is prone to anxiety or sadness. Going through a crisis such as a breakup or a loss does not help either. But even in the absence of extra challenges, concentrating on the breath for longer than a few minutes is not easy at the beginning. Guided meditations are helpful, as, every few minutes—hopefully just when the beginner's concentration is waning—there is a reminder that moves the meditation forward. After several guided meditations, silent meditation becomes easier, as you remember some of the instructions you heard in previous sessions, and can use these to guide yourself.

Here are a few other differences between rumination and meditation:

> *Rumination keeps us in the box—the box we know as our "self."*
> *Meditation moves us out of the box toward open vistas.*
> *Rumination reinforces our mental habits, as we keep going round and round the same ground.*
> *Meditation frees us from entrenched habits.*
> *No concentration is needed for rumination. It happens automatically.*
> *Concentration is needed for meditation—we need to stay on track.*
> *No guidance is needed for rumination.*

Recognize the times when you slip into rumination mode, and come back to your breath and to the here and now. It is normal to occasionally slip into short periods of rumination at the beginning. Come back to observing your breath as soon as you recognize what is happening. With time, you will catch yourself sooner, and time spent ruminating will diminish. Another way to short-circuit rumination is writing.

2. WRITE AND MOVE ON

If you have a lot on your mind, alternate periods of silent sitting with writing. It is possible to mentally repeat the sentence "He is so mean" many times when ruminating, but you are not likely to write down a whole page of it when journaling. Writing helps move you through obstinate thoughts. When ruminating we start from zero each time. When writing, we usually go from where we stopped the last time. If you are writing, the thought "He is so mean" will probably be expressed differently the next time it shows up—perhaps with a different nuance, perhaps with an extra insight. And when you turn a page, you really turn a page.

As you write, your fleeting thoughts will turn into moments of self-knowledge or plans of action. Your notebook can become an intimate friend, sometimes more intimate than any "real" friend. You may find that you confide things to it that you have not revealed to anyone. Thoughts are like bubbles on a flowing river—they float away without leaving a trace. Thoughts that are written down do leave a trace. Just articulating a half-conscious question makes it easier to go toward finding the answer.

Thich Nhat Hanh sometimes recommends writing therapeutic letters that you may never send. Those letters may be to your father, your lover, or your boss. Henry David Thoreau's journal was his constant companion, and the source of that intimate flavor we so appreciate in his writing.

My own practice is to write *after* a period of meditation. A period of meditation often gets my creative juices flowing.

3. MEDITATE TO GAIN SELF-KNOWLEDGE

"Knowing others is wisdom, knowing oneself is enlightenment," says the *Tao Te Ching*. Knowing oneself includes being aware of our patterns of behavior, our habits, and our tendencies. These do not always make us—or those around us—happy.

Usually, our focus is outward: we are responding to work demands, navigating traffic, or making earth-shaking decisions in the kitchen. Periods of meditation turn our focus inward so that we are left alone with ourselves. This voluntary aloneness is different from social aloneness, which might be involuntary, or mixed with feelings of boredom. Even if you are meditating with a group, you are still alone with yourself because you are not interacting with others socially.

Our daily life provides fodder for meditation periods. There are many "aha!" moments in meditation. Insights germinate underground during the day or night, and burst into our awareness during meditation periods. Meditation is a way of honoring this process by making time and space for it. It may look like you are doing nothing while sitting in meditation, but do not be misled by appearances: it also looks like nothing is happening for quite a while after you seed your garden in the spring.

4. EMBRACE CHANGE

Noticing that you habitually react with anger or anxiety is an important step, but do not stop there. Many people do. They get to "I'm this way," and they park there. They discount the plasticity of the brain, and the plasticity of habits. I would not have written this book if I did not have firsthand knowledge that making intentional changes in my own habits has been possible. This gave me the courage to promote voluntary change in others. I have seen this kind of beneficial change happen again and again.

If you get nothing else from reading this book, please take this one word with you. That word is "YES!" Yes, you can change in ways that bring happiness to you and to others around you. Mindfulness is a practice that promotes change. "Paying attention intentionally" is one definition of mindfulness. Let us add "continuously" to this to make the definition, "Mindfulness is paying attention intentionally and continuously." By catching yourself before a habit takes over, you provide the space for changing that habit, one instance after another. But patience and persistence are also essential. Do not expect a habit you have formed over twenty years or more to change overnight. Now you are like a musician practicing the guitar. Your body is the guitar, your fingers are your mindfulness, and the song you wish to play is the song of happiness.

Mahatma Gandhi said, "Be the change you wish to see in the world." For this discussion, let us revise that to read, "Be the change you wish to see in yourself."

5. MEDITATE FOR CREATIVITY

When you mentally revisit a challenging situation, you may find that your understanding of it has changed a little bit. That is because the brain works on things behind the scenes. The unconscious mind comes up with suggestions that are sometimes ingenious, and sometimes nonsensical. The conscious mind accepts and hones what is offered or rejects what it finds inappropriate. Creative thinking is a conversation. Different parts of the brain work together in a friendly way. The unconscious mind may be like the night owl, going to work when the rest of you goes to sleep. Or it can be like the genie that lies bottled up inside you. Every once in a while it comes alive, stirs up its cloudy body, and spills out of the bottle. The genie obeys its own schedule, which is difficult to pin down and put on the Google calendar. We can create the right conditions for it, but we cannot force creativity.

Turn your life into a poem! Create the conditions so that the genie and the night owl can work with you! Tame the talking head inside by adding a dose of meditation, of breath and body awareness! Practice brainstorming instead of getting caught up in brainstorms! Use meditation to make space for creativity.

6. USE INTENTION

We go through many mental states as each day unfolds. This allows us to respond to the challenges of each moment appropriately—you need a different mental state to get out of the way of an oncoming car than you do for enjoying a cup of coffee with friends! Letting go of the previous moment is the only way to be in *this* moment.

When mental states are stubborn or sticky, it is usually because they are nourished by thoughts. If you are angry with Sean, and you keep bringing to mind all your reasons for being mad at him over and over, it is not surprising that your anger continues unabated. On the other hand, if you are in love with him, and keep thinking loving thoughts about him, then it is your love that stays with you.

123

In the above examples, you do not make an effort to think angry or loving thoughts about Sean. These thoughts seem to happen automatically, and keep you stuck in a certain state of mind. You can do the same thing intentionally—you can direct your thoughts whichever way you want.

❁

Martin came to see me for meditation coaching. Among other things, he complained about having negative thoughts about himself. Lately these thoughts had become more insistent and strident, and he was having trouble keeping them at bay. My suggestion to him was not to fight with these thoughts—if we struggle to keep negative thoughts away, they become stronger and stronger. "Do not wrestle or box with them," I suggested. "Instead, fill your mind with positive thoughts about yourself." I asked him to visualize a young child of three, four, or five—a charming and lovable child. He was that child once. That lovely boy is still in him. I asked him to fill his heart with love and admiration for that young boy, and to move gradually toward focusing on himself at the present time. "As you fill your heart with positive thoughts about yourself, there will be no room for negative thoughts. Your heart will be overflowing with positive thoughts.

"Do this practice regularly every day," I told him. "Once is not enough." This is an example where "filling the mind" can be a better metaphor for meditation than the more usual "emptying the mind."

We can use intention both for letting go, and for hanging on. We can let go of stress, and we can hang on to relaxation. Our thoughts and activities leave behind a lingering aroma in the mind. It is like the smells in the kitchen. Clear the air by opening the windows or turning on the exhaust fan if the kitchen is full of the smell of fried onions or burnt toast. But hang on to the lingering smell of cinnamon apple pie.

7. REDEFINE PRAYER

In theistic religions, prayer is a deep wish addressed to God.

But prayer can also be a deep wish addressed to *ourselves*—a deep wish coming from our conscious self, to the energy that runs our lives, makes our hearts beat, puts us to sleep, and wakes us up.

"May I always be true to myself."

"May the choices I make each moment reflect my concern for the environment."

"May I remember to keep a smile in my heart."

These are examples of prayerlike vows. We ourselves are the entity responsible for making our deepest wishes come true. No one else can do it for us. Articulating, writing down, or repeating our vows helps us to print them on our hearts. It reminds us to take steps toward their fulfillment.

8. "VACCINATE YOURSELF" WITH SERENITY MEDITATION

Casually clicking on the preset buttons on my car radio recently, I heard about the worrisome effects of the downturn in the Chinese stock market, the refugee crisis in Europe, and how global warming has now reached a point of no return, all in the space of a few minutes. If these news items seem outdated by the time you read this, there will certainly be other anxiety-provoking stories to take their place. We are living in an age of anxiety, and the prevailing global anxiety adds to our feelings about our jobs, our families, our bank accounts, and the state of our health. Anxiety feels like the new normal. Serenity meditation is a necessary antidote for this "environmental toxin." It helps bring balance to our lives.

If we are traveling to a country where malaria is common, we take some kind of antitoxin to counter the danger. Serenity meditation is like that medicine. We do not have malaria in the West—we have anxiety. We need a daily dose of serenity meditation in order to counteract it.

There is no meditation without calming the mind. It is the starting point, and the gate to the kingdom. All the suggestions mentioned above begin with calming the mind. Whatever your state of mind when you start—whether you are upset, stressed, in need of inspiration, having trouble sleeping, or if you just want to "chill out"—sit in the meditation posture and get in touch with your breath. Breathe in and out slowly—five or six seconds in, and five or six seconds out. And go from there.

Time for Practice

Guided Meditation: Reducing Rumination

In Zen, a person going round and round in her thoughts is compared to a ghost clinging to bushes and grasses. Notice when you tend to ruminate during the day, and create strategies for shortening these periods. For me, the challenge was during that slippery time between waking up and getting up. The snooze button on the alarm? It was my Ruminate Button. Now I'm more aware of what my mind is doing. If an insight is emerging as I wake up, I honor it by writing it down. If there is no insight, I often make room for it by sitting up for morning meditation. This is an opportunity to open up to creativity.

When do you tend to ruminate? Is it when you go to bed at night? Is it when you drive? Is it when bad things happen? Find ways to prevent rumination from taking over your mind.

I take a few deep breaths.
Deep, conscious breaths clear my mind.
I continue to keep my mind clear by concentrating on each
*   breath.*

❦

When I think,
am I just juggling words, or is thinking more than juggling
*   words?*

Words are labels for people, ideas, and things.
But there is more to a person than her label.
A person is not just her name.
Similarly, the reality of an idea is different from its label.

❀

"Words!" I say to myself, when I find my mind juggling them.
I let go of the words that crowd my mind.
Words make the unknown appear familiar.
They make us feel that we know more than we actually do.

❀

Words do not mean anything by themselves.
A Chinese word I do not understand does not mean anything
*   to me.*
Neither does a random name from a list.
Words get their meaning from what they stand for.

❀

What is the reality behind each name, each label?
As a word crosses my mind,
*   I slow down, and touch that reality.*

❀

If repetitive thoughts persist, I open my eyes wide for a while.
I lock on something,
*   and rest my gaze there without letting my eyes wander.*
The object is not important. The steady gaze is important.
I keep my eyes open for several breaths.
There is less room for repetitive thoughts when the eyes are open.

❀

I can also mentally sing a mindfulness song that I remember.
Like a bird perched on my shoulder,
a mindfulness song keeps reminding me of my focus.

❊

Then, I let go of the song, and stay in the space the song created.
I continue to enjoy the rhythmic sensations of my breathing.

Many people focus on thinking, or overthinking, as the problem during meditation.

With this exercise I want to change the focus from "thinking" to "words."

It is possible to think without words: ever since I was a young boy, I have been thinking musically—with melodies and harmonies. I imagine that visual artists think in shapes and colors.

Try catching your mental energy before it becomes words. Try to breathe with the energy for a while. Then find a creative way to express it—with words, if necessary, as a poem, but also in action or in some other way.

Practice Song: Birds of Joy

Birds of joy, birds of sadness
Sing their songs all day long,
I hear them sing, I smile and breathe,
And keep my heart free and strong.

This song does not deny that circumstances affect us. It acknowledges hearing the songs of the birds, the voices of our feelings. Being open to feeling things deeply is what makes us human—feelings are the muse of poetry and song, and the engine of empathy and compassion. But there is nothing pretty or poetic about getting lost in emotions, or drowning in sorrow. The depressed people I know are not writing poetry or helping others. They are in need of help and inspiration themselves. There is a difference between being moved by emotions, and falling into an emotional pit.

By their very nature, emotions tend to grab us. They are both mental and visceral—they can take over our bodies as well as our minds. When we let that happen, there is nothing left outside the space of the emotion, no ground to stand on, and we lose objectivity.

Chapter 9

Appreciate What You Have

Time for a Story

. . . .

The Most Important Moment

The Dalai Lama was once asked, "What was the most important moment of your life?"

Perhaps the interviewer was expecting something like "When I was invested with the title of the Fourteenth Dalai Lama at the age of fifteen" or "When I escaped from Tibet."

But he simply replied, "It is right now."

Time for Reflection

. . . .

Many people are alive but don't touch the miracle
of being alive.
—THICH NHAT HANH

Imagine yourself in an apple orchard. Apples everywhere, hundreds, thousands of them.

Yet, you can only eat one apple at a time. You pick it—you feel the firmness and that characteristic shape in your hand. As you bring it to your mouth, there is a certain fresh smell. You take a bite, and hear the crunchy sound.

Ahh, that familiar taste.

You walk on a beach—there are billions of grains of sand all around. But you feel only the handful that are under your feet at each step.

Time is also like that. It may be endless, eternal, infinite, and whatever else poets and physicists like to call it. Yet it is only this moment that we experience now; we only experience one slice of it at a time.

The shape, feel, characteristic smell, and taste of the apple are part of what the Zen tradition calls the suchness of the apple, of *this* apple. Words do not do justice to it. Times of day—the early morning, sunset, and the full moon at night—also have their suchness. Each moment does, flavored by the people and whatever else it contains.

Memories, Regrets, Abstractions

Mental phenomena have a mesmerizing effect on us. The effect is almost hypnotic—in the previous chapter I called it the Pied Piper effect, because we tend to follow them despite ourselves.

Coming to our senses is a good way to escape this effect. If you are gripped by regret, dwelling on it will only bring more pain. It will not solve anything.

We all grow. In retrospect, yesterday's actions appear immature today—that is an inevitable side effect of growth. The momentary pain of regret—the pangs—may be inevitable, but the prolonged suffering is optional.

Start by noticing that you are breathing. Continue by noticing all the sensations in your body. Make a tour of all five senses, but do not just do a quick check and go back to wandering through the deep wells and the cobwebs of the mind. Stay with sensual awareness. The blue sky and the flowers on the table are the answers to life's problems. They are the answers to life's puzzles. Life is not only a question; it is also the answer—the only answer. The blue sky and the flowers point to the suchness of things, and that is all there is.

Mindfulness for Believers

Without some part of ourselves that sees beyond the narrowly etched boundary of the self and considers the larger picture and its interests and needs, we can all be very destructive. Brothers and sisters can destroy one another, a couple can destroy each other, a politician can destroy her country, and a corporation can destroy the environment.

I know this intimately: as a child, the bullying of my older brother gave me a lot of heartache.

The ego looks after the self.

What is the entity that looks after the family, the community, and the environment?

For enlightened believers, this has sometimes been God. "Enlightened" is the important word here—for we have too often seen the Muslim God fighting the Christian God and the Jewish God. Unfortunately, as God no longer has arms and legs as during the ancient Greek times, He now uses human arms to hold the gun and human fingers to pull the trigger.

Many believers have transcended the boundaries of race and culture, and have brought solace to people who needed it. Mother Teresa, Martin Luther King, Jr., and Gregory Boyle, the founder of Homeboy Industries in Los Angeles, are inspiring examples.

If you're a believer, mindfulness can be that transcendent part of you—the part that transcends the narrow boundaries of the personal self and connects with the source of love and peace. This is mindfulness of God, for a God of whom you are not mindful is not going to be a strong presence in your life. Believers also need mindfulness.

Mindfulness itself is a practice, and it works with or without beliefs. It is the practice of bringing ideals, values, dreams—whatever you hold dear—down to Earth. If you are a believer, remember that God also came down to Earth. With mindfulness, every day is Christmas, and every moment has the joyful feel of a Christmas carol.

Having and Enjoying

"My wealth is not possession but enjoyment," wrote Henry David Thoreau.

Possession and enjoyment are not always synonymous. It is by enjoying what we have that we become happier, not by having more. That is because we tend to take our possessions, our gifts, and our blessings for granted. Your big toe has been there since you were born. How much do you enjoy having it?

But it is when you stub it and it hurts that you become aware of it. To enjoy what we have, we must be aware of what we have. Do not wait for the pain. Seize the blessing of the moment instead. Appreciate your wholeness this moment, for this moment is all you have. If you do not have this moment, you do not have anything.

Gem in the Hem

There is a parable in the Lotus Sutra, a much-beloved Buddhist text, where a rich man discreetly tries to help out a friend who is not doing so well. He sews a very valuable gem into the hem of his jacket, without telling him. His friend does not know this, and some time later falls into even harder times. He lives in poverty and misery despite unknowingly carrying around this treasure every day. One day, the two old friends meet again. The rich man is surprised to see his friend living in poverty. He undoes the hem of his friend's jacket, and shows him the priceless gem he has been unknowingly carrying around all this time.

We are all rich, but many of us do not know it, and continue to live as if we are poor. I assume that everybody who reads this book has the gift of life, although some may be unaware of it. Awareness of this gift goes by various names such as Gratitude, Wisdom, Awakening, and Enlightenment. Enlightenment? Yes, for I cannot imagine an enlightened person who spends his days feeling miserably unhappy.

We have the conditions for happiness sewn into the fabric of our genes and our life on Earth, but our culture neglects to tell us this. We need to discover it through mindfulness.

Know What You've Got Now, Before It's Gone

This revised line from a Joni Mitchell song could be the motto for the practice of happiness. I decided to modify Mitchell's words slightly for the purpose of this chapter, since the original, "You don't know what you got till it's gone," is not always true—the Buddha knew it, Thich Nhat Hanh knows it, and, thanks to them, I know it also. Not only just the three of us, but many others have the gift of recognizing their blessings and appreciating them. Countless others have learned this through their life experiences. It is my deep wish that this book will be a channel for spreading this precious knowledge wider.

More Parables

Paulo Coelho's *The Alchemist* is the story of a shepherd boy named Santiago. The story starts at dusk as Santiago arrives with his flock of sheep at an abandoned church somewhere in Andalusia, in the south of Spain. "The roof had fallen in long ago, and an enormous sycamore had grown on the spot where the sacristy had once stood."

Remember these words, for the story comes back to this scene at the end, after Santiago travels through Morocco, the Sahara desert, and parts of Egypt in search of his dream and his heart's treasure. In the course of his adventures, within sight of the pyramids, he learns that the treasure he has been seeking is buried under that sycamore tree, in the abandoned church where the story started. It had been there all the time, but he did not know it.

The story is rich in details. One detail I appreciate is that during the course of his adventures he meets the woman he has been longing for, but he is advised by the alchemist not to marry her and settle down prematurely before he realizes his dream. To do so would be abandoning the dream, and settling down to a humdrum existence. The alchemist's advice turns out to be the right advice, as, in the end, he gets both his dream and the woman he loves.

Here are the final words of the story, after he has dug the huge treasure of old Spanish gold coins from under that sycamore tree:

"'I'm coming, Fatima,' he said."

He had not forgotten her.

(Be forewarned: if you decide to read this short novella, make sure that you have a couple of free hours ahead of you, for you will not be able to put it down!)

A story by the Hassidic master Rabbi Nachman of Breslov makes a similar point in a parable titled *The Treasure*:

A poor Jew who lived in the city of Prague dreamed that he should journey to Vienna because there was a buried treasure waiting for him under a bridge leading to the king's palace. The dream kept recurring, so he decided to go there and try to dig out this treasure. When he arrived, he saw that some soldiers were guarding the bridge. He stayed around, waiting for an opportunity when the guards were not paying attention, but they soon grew suspicious and confronted him. The Jew told them the story of his dream. One of the soldiers started laughing at him sarcastically. He said that believing in dreams was foolish—just last night he had dreamt that a poor Jew in Prague had a treasure buried in his cellar, and that the soldier should go and dig for that treasure, but he was too intelligent to believe in such silly things and to take dreams seriously. The soldier even had the Jew's home address right!

The Jew turned back and hurried home, dug in his cellar, and found the treasure.

I like to think that his relationship with his wife was part of the treasure he found—perhaps he started seeing his wife in a new light and began to treasure her. Perhaps this was part of his awakening. The soldier guarding the bridge, on the other hand, is an example of the type of person who does not value his dreams.

There are three common motifs to these stories:

First, the treasure of happiness is already here where we are, under our feet or almost in our pocket—it is just that we do not realize it. We do not appreciate what we already have.

We may live mindlessly, walking, driving, and working without paying attention, without being fully present. We may listen half-heartedly to our children and to our partner while we think of other things. We may breathe without appreciating the miracle of being alive.

Mindfulness is the practice of waking up to life, and appreciating this priceless treasure we all possess.

Second, we need to make a journey of discovery, a pilgrimage, or a "trip" of some kind before we learn to appreciate what we already have. There is the suffering of ignorance first. We need to go somewhere else on a quest so that we can come back and connect with the treasure that was under our feet all along. This was certainly true in my case—I participated in Zen retreats and spent nearly a year in Plum Village as I slowly absorbed the practice of mindfulness. Many seekers of my generation went to India on this search. Others tried drugs, and many lost their way. In the end what is gained and what is found is nothing special—we still eat, breathe, and walk.

Third, we usually do not know precisely what we are seeking. To some extent, this is inevitable, for in order to know what we seek accurately and in detail we have to have found it in the first place!

This was true of Santiago in *The Alchemist*, and it is a feature of Paulo Coelho's writing that the journey of seeking itself and being faithful to the journey are important in themselves. Again, this was true in my case—at one time I was quite taken by Yoga and Indian spirituality, then I was seduced by all the Zen rhetoric about awakening without having any clear idea of what it was. I'm glad that I did not give up my search, for that is how I eventually discovered the practice of mindfulness and the Buddhist teachings around it. Recently this has been true of some of the people who take my Mindfulness Training for Stress Reduction and Personal Growth classes. They may have initially enrolled in order to reduce their stress or anxiety levels, but some of the participants changed goals midstream to embrace the practice of mindfulness and its connection to happiness.

Being here now is essential for feeling happy and contented, for appreciation of the good things of life will elude us if we are not present to enjoy them. The sky might be a gorgeous blue, and the trees may have their best dresses on, but if we are not there to appreciate these and other wonders around us, we will not experience a feeling of happiness. When we aren't there, it is as if they aren't there also—it is as if there is nothing to be happy about. Mindfulness helps create happiness more than riches and success, for it helps us to enjoy these things. We will not be contented if we are not aware of the sources of our contentment. Without mindfulness, we may even feel that we have nothing to be happy about, because we aren't in touch with the present moment and all its treasures.

However, mindfulness is not only noticing the beauty around and within us, and hurrying on. Our attention needs to keep up as "now" evolves with time, and "here" evolves with space. Mindfulness is more than a momentary glance at the here and now. It is continuous attention to everything we experience, do, or say. It is being there as we walk or enjoy a cup of coffee; it is doing things wholeheartedly and with attention. That way, we "own" our experience. We own it not in a possessive sense, but in the sense of being committed to it. Without that, a sense of contentment and happiness might not arise. The same enjoyable things and experiences may still be there, but we are not there to enjoy them and feel the contentment and happiness that they bring. It is the difference between barely noticing the daylight when the alarm goes off, and basking in the sunlight in the park on a bright day. It is the difference between dashing to your car on a hot day, and taking the time to enjoy the warmth of the sun on a beach. With mindfulness, body and mind regain their unity; we notice things not only as a ghost might, but we also enjoy them as fully embodied humans, with our minds, bodies, and emotions.

Indeed, the metaphor of the ghost is an appropriate one. A ghost does not have a body. As we hurry on from one thing to another, our attention is often on a mental plane, and sometimes not even that—if we are thinking of other things as we go through our routines. We may be driving, walking, and eating as a ghost would. With mindfulness, the ghost becomes embodied as her body and mind become one with her experience, and contentment becomes possible. In the Buddhist tradition, we speak of hungry ghosts, not contented ghosts. A ghost presumably feels craving, hunger, and envy on a mental level, but not satisfaction or contentment, for those are feelings that require a body to realize them.

Hello, Charlie Brown!

The fact that we are all doomed to get old, sick, and die preconditions all of us to anxiety. Add to that uncertainty about if we are doing the right thing, are following the right career, or have chosen the right life companion. It is easy to fall into the anxiety trap. The cartoon character Charlie Brown often expressed anxiety in musings such as, "I think I'm afraid to be happy because whenever I get too happy, something bad always happens." Do you also have an inner Charlie Brown? Recognize his voice when he speaks, and smile! Acknowledge his contribution to your day! Thank your inner CB for his gloomy comments and move on!

Dying Happy

Despite everything in the last paragraph, it is possible to die happy. The poet William Blake died in exemplary fashion. On the day of his death (August 12, 1827), Blake kept working on his book on Dante. Eventually, it is reported, he stopped working and turned to his wife, who was in tears by his bedside. As he looked at her, Blake said, "Hold it, Kate! Stay just as you are, I want to draw your portrait, for you have ever been an angel to me." Blake was a visual artist as well as a poet. Having completed the portrait, he laid down his tools and began to sing hymns and verses. Blake died later in the evening, after promising his wife that he would always be with her. A woman who was staying with them later said, "I have been at the death, not of a man, but of a blessed angel."

Blake wrote, "He whose face gives no light shall never become a star." He continued to give light until the end. I would not mind dying like that. Many of the elements of positivity that I discuss in this book are there: singing inspirational songs that fill one's heart with positive emotions, continuing to do something that gives meaning to your life until the last moment—there is no talk of "retirement" here—and the ability and the willingness to keep a relationship alive as long as he was alive. Note that there is not a word of complaining here—if there was any discomfort or pain, he kept it to himself. And the miracle is that he was offering sweet thoughts to Kate, his love, and filling her heart with positivity even as he himself was dying.

Another exemplary story of death is about the recent passing of Pete Seeger. It is recounted by Peter Yarrow of Peter, Paul and Mary fame. As Yarrow tells it, one day he, as well as some other folk singers who had walked the same path and sang the same songs as Seeger, were asked to come over, as his family felt that the end was near. Yarrow recounts an afternoon filled with Seeger favorites such as "We Shall Overcome" and "Where Have All the Flowers Gone?" as Pete listened with a blissful smile from his bed. Then he went to sleep. He later died in his sleep at around nine thirty.

Time for Practice

. . . .

Guided Meditation: The Light of Consciousness

❀

Focus on your breath.
It's the body that breathes.
Let the mind join the body in breathing.

❀

The mind often takes you for a ride.
It takes you to places familiar and unfamiliar.
Stay with your breath, and watch your mind in action.
Notice the kind of thoughts that spontaneously pop up in
*   your mind.*
Notice what they are about.
Observe their feeling tone:
Are they loving thoughts, anxious thoughts, angry
*   thoughts . . . ?*

❀

Now consider your goals and values,
*   where you want to be in two years.*
Are these spontaneously occurring thoughts likely to get you
*   there,*

or do you need new mental habits as travel companions?
The first step in changing our mental habits is deciding to
  change them,
but this is not enough. We also need practice.
We need to create new tracks for the mind to follow.

❀

Practice being proactive now.
If your mind's habitual chatter is not in accord with your
  values,
do not just listen passively.
Instead, express your values, and let your mind listen.
Learn to talk back to your mind.
As soon as you hear its familiar voice, take over.
This is conscious habit formation.

❀

We can steer the direction of our thoughts just like we steer a car:
Shine the headlights of the car on whatever you fancy now.
Practice directing the light of consciousness voluntarily.
Find what is beautiful and nourishing in your environment;
Shine the light of your consciousness on that.
Steer your mind toward bright and agreeable vistas.
Steer it toward happiness.

❀

You are the light you yearn for.
Feel your light, be the light.

Practice Song: Be Here Now

Be here now, now, the sun is warm, the sky is blue,
Be here now, now, and hold my hand in yours.

The sun only shines, the wind only blows,
Love only warms in the here and now, in the here
  and now.
Tomorrow is a seed in the garden of time,
It will flower, it will bloom if we garden with care,
In the here and now.

Chapter 10

Take Care of Yourself

Time for a Story

. . . .

Take Care of Yourself

Once there was a father-and-daughter team of street entertainers who earned their living by performing acrobatic acts. First, the father balanced a ten-foot pole on his head. Then, the young girl climbed on him, stepping on his knees, hands, and shoulders, and finally going to the top of the pole. Just when the watchers started applauding enthusiastically, the father would start walking round and round while the girl maintained perfect balance—a very tricky act requiring complete concentration on the part of both.

The father was proud of his daughter. "We succeed so well because when we are performing, I take care of you and you take care of me," he said to her affectionately.

The daughter was surprised. "No, Papa," she said. "If we did what you say, we would both fall down in the middle of our act. We succeed because I take care of me, and you take care of you."

Time for Reflection

. . . .

Who is rich? The one who appreciates what he has.
—THE TALMUD

No matter what is going on in your life, even when you feel like you are balancing on a ten-foot pole resting precariously on someone's head, your primary responsibility is to yourself. No one else can help you on that ten-foot pole.

Perhaps you are faced with aging or sick parents, children who need attention, and a problem boss at work. Neither that boss, your children, or your sick parents can take care of you—they are probably all struggling to keep their own heads above water. Taking care of you is your responsibility, your "file."

Camille, a participant in one of my Sleep Better with Mindfulness Meditation groups, was again complaining about the way her boss spoke to her at work. He seemed to be always full of anger, and everything he said came out angry. That bothered Camille, especially when she tried to go to sleep at night.

We discussed her options, and agreed that there was not much she could do about his state of mind. Then I asked her if his state of mind was her responsibility, her "file." I saw that she did not quite get what I meant by that, because she replied with a torrent of "He should not speak like that, he should not do that." So, I tried another tack. I said that she should not drive the car she had; instead she should sell it, and buy another make and model. She should also not shop at the grocery store she usually goes to, but instead go to another chain. She should also change her hairdo. She stopped her complaints, and looked at me as if I had come from another planet. I saw that she felt that these things were none of my business, they were not my files. I explained to her that the state of mind of her boss was also not her file. It might have been, if she had been a psychotherapist and the boss had come to her for therapy, but that was not the case now. Even then, her concern with his state of mind would properly be limited to the therapy hour.

Assuming control of someone else's files may create conflict at work. If you are a welfare officer, and you walk over to a coworker's filing cabinet, pick up one of her files, and start making phone calls, you are heading for trouble! The heart of the problem is that you do not have ultimate or legitimate control over someone else's business. If the situation in the welfare office came to light, you would be the guilty party. You would not be helping anyone—instead, you would be creating confusion.

Attempting to assume control over what is properly someone else's problem creates a similar kind of mayhem. Yes, the state of mind of your boss affects you. But so does the weather. You react to the weather by taking along an umbrella, or by dressing appropriately—not by trying to change it. How you react to the weather is your responsibility, not the weather itself. A similar division of responsibility holds in relation to your boss. How you react to what he says or does is your business, not what he says or does. (This is, of course, within limits. If your boss crosses the line into legally abusive behavior, that is another matter.)

You *need* to take care of your own well-being, just like you have to take care of your own files at work. Have compassion for your grumpy boss and her family—her spouse and children have to put up with her all the time, including through the weekends and during bedtime. You are free from her during bedtime—unless you carry her to bed in your head. However, she is the one who suffers most from her grumpiness. Her grumpiness limits her vision and her enjoyment of life 24/7.

Mindfulness can be your guide here. Remind yourself constantly that your boss's grumpiness is about him, not about you. Taking things personally may be a habit you picked up as a child—in order to make children aware of their responsibilities, parents often say things like, "It is your fault if you failed that course. You never did any homework." Some carry this kind of guilt-tripping too far. Mindfulness meditation helps us sort out where our feelings come from. This is a great help for finding peace of mind. The *source* of our feelings is inside us. What happens outside us serves merely as a *trigger*. To see this clearly brings consolation.

To come back to the welfare office metaphor on the previous page, important as it is for a caseworker to stay out of other people's business, it is also important for her to take care of her own files conscientiously. What are Camille's own responsibilities in this case? They are her own attitude and peace of mind.

Rudyard Kipling summarized Camille's task in a poem titled "If":

> If you can keep your head when all about you
> Are losing theirs and blaming it on you,
> If you can trust yourself when all men doubt you,
> But make allowance for their doubting too;
>
> If you can wait and not be tired by waiting,
> Or being lied about, don't deal in lies,
> Or being hated, don't give way to hating,
> And yet don't look too good, nor talk too wise . . .
> Yours is the Earth and everything that's in it . . .

Kipling's conclusion points out the importance he placed on this skill.

The issue is the ability to resist being contaminated by other people's moods, and to resist taking others' words personally. What others say reflects their state of mind—it is about them, and not about you. Not being bothered by others' moods is equanimity.

Stress is a contributing cause of many illnesses, including heart disease, cancer, and multiple sclerosis. Stress does not stay only in the mind, because mind and body are not separate. By taking care of our mental states, we are also taking care of our body. The converse is also true, and during the rest of this chapter, I would like to say a few things about the care of the body.

Basics of Healthy Living

Of all our possessions, the most precious is undoubtedly our body. We *are* our body. We will enjoy our house, car, or smartphone more if we have a healthy body. Having money creates a sense of entitlement, but beware: our body is not impressed by that sense of entitlement—one cannot order one's body around forever. One cannot say to the body, "Here, eat this fried food, drink this sugary pop, smoke this cigarette, and be happy" for long, and get away with it.

In this chapter, I would like to go over three essentials of physical well-being. All the previous chapters have focused on mental aspects of happiness. Yet, the well-being of our body is intimately connected with how happy we feel.

We do take care of the body—but often we only take care of its appearance. We spend money on clothes, on cosmetics, on beauty salons, and on plastic surgery. None of that does any good to our health, extends our life span, or prevents illness. It is like waxing a car that really needs an oil change.

At the Supermarket

It turns out that we do not get fat because we overeat.

Rather, the opposite is true—we overeat because we are fat.

And we become fat by eating the wrong kind of foods.

Dr. David Ludwig explains in his book *Always Hungry?* that we metabolize carbohydrates as sugar. A high-carbohydrate diet increases the level of the hormone insulin in the bloodstream. This, in turn, makes our fat cells store calories as fat. Then there is a shortage of sugar in the bloodstream. This makes the brain send out hunger signals so that we can eat and replenish those missing calories. And the cycle continues. Willpower? Mindfulness? The brain runs on sugar. When this metabolic disorder depletes the sugar available to the brain, the brain is no longer running at its best. Those desirable energies are weakened when we most need them. We can break this cycle by eating a balanced diet with less carbohydrates, less added sugar, and more fats, protein, and fiber. What we eat turns out to be more important than just counting calories.

It is said that one cube of sugar in the gas tank is enough to ruin the engine of a car. We would not put it there. Added sugar is just as harmful for the human body, yet we do put it there. Added sugar is omnipresent on the supermarket shelves even in unexpected places such as in instant beef gravy (24 percent), and in Worcestershire sauce (10 percent). You can only avoid it, or at least keep it within bounds, by remembering to check the labels of everything you buy, even if you need a magnifying glass to do it. With habitual consumption of added sugar, "sweet" begins to taste normal, and everything that is not sweetened tastes a little flat. It is like wearing colored eyeglasses.

Sugar is addictive. The food industry puts it in everything so that you eat more of everything. But they are not doing you a favor. Here is one effect of high sugar consumption you may not have heard about: studies confirm that heavy sugar consumption leads to an increased risk of depression and worse outcomes in schizophrenia. Sugar causes inflammation, which has an adverse effect on the brain and also on the immune system. Countries with high sugar consumption also have higher rates of depression.

You can discover the effect of sugar on your emotional state for yourself. An effective way to do this is to stay away from added sugar for a few weeks, and then have a generous helping. For the full effect, have your sugary treat by itself, without food, perhaps in the form of a can of pop or a handful of candies or both. Monitor how you feel afterward.

Mindfulness is necessary at the food store. Our first source of food was our mother. We trusted her implicitly and we thrived. We continue to trust people who offer us food; food is part of hospitality. There are blessings, grace before meals, and songs of gratitude associated with food. Forget all that when you enter a supermarket. Unfortunately, there is nothing blessed about the food industry these days. The front of a typical packaged food item says **GOOD FOR YOU!** in big letters and smiling pictures, while the list of ingredients on the back says *unhealthy* in small print and confusing language.

At the Dining Table

When I sit at the table, my stomach says, "More, more, I'm famished." I follow its advice. Then, at some point, it changes its tune and starts saying, "Oh, you ate too much. I'm stuffed!" There is no middle ground. My stomach never says, "You ate just enough, now stop." It's either not enough or too much. Rather, it's both, one after the other. That makes it hard to follow the solid nutritional advice that says, "Eat until you are three-quarters full." When I'm filling up my water bottle, I see what I'm doing—I can stop at three quarters if I want to. When I'm eating, I do not see how full the stomach is, and the feelings from the stomach are not reliable.

The odd thing is that often I eat not because I'm hungry, but because it's time to. Being late for a meal feels like being late for an appointment. And appetite often comes, or is intensified, as I start to eat. Some time ago, I wondered what would happen if I faced this situation head-on, and sat down to eat less frequently.

Two Meals a Day?: An Experiment

Buddha ate only one meal a day. In case you think that this was because he was not given to sensual indulgence, so did the Romans, who *were* given to sensual indulgence. Food historian Caroline

Yeldham writes, "The Romans believed it was healthier to eat only one meal a day." Reay Tannahill, in his *Food in History*, notes that until the time of Louis XIV, the French ate only two meals a day.

I decided to give the two-meals-a-day program a try.

I followed it for several months. In the process, I lost some weight and learned to make friends with the feeling of hunger. Learning to feel urges without indulging in them is one of the things one learns through meditation. Yet, this is not so easy to do at the dinner table. There, the stomach conspires with the brain, and its messages for having second helpings or extra dessert feel like brilliant ideas. I do not blame anybody for being fooled. For me, it was easier to sit at the dining table less often than resist once I was there.

After several months of this, something changed. My stomach and brain became convinced that I could survive and thrive on less food. Indeed, I was feeling better all around. I was learning to accept hunger as a normal sensation instead of as an emergency that needs to be fixed urgently. Accepting hunger is an important step. It allows us to give our digestive system a rest. Reducing our meal frequency is not mentioned in any books on weight loss that I have come across. I have not heard it discussed on *The Dr. Oz Show*. Yet, it meets the challenge head-on. The challenge is accepting hunger without immediately wanting to eat something. We learn to meet this kind of challenge in other areas as we learn to feel anger without bashing someone's face in. We learn to feel sleepy without immediately making ourselves comfortable on the office floor for a nap. Learning to be comfortable with the feeling of hunger is also helpful for weight loss. My experience also taught me that this is a temporary condition—we get used to two meals a day after a while, and it becomes the new normal.

It's All in Your Gut

Once upon a time, when it came to things like stress and unhappiness, people claimed, "It's all in your head." Now, more and more people are saying, "It's all in your gut." It turns out that the microbes in the gut have a hand in determining how we feel; they also influence whether we are thin or overweight. It is now becoming clear that we need to eat to nourish not only ourselves but our gut microbes as well. And chief among the delicacies those little critters crave is fiber. Beware of juices of all kinds—there is more nutrition in the discarded pulp than in the juice. Best to eat the whole fruit or whole vegetable rather than just drink the sugary juice.

This is our life. It is the most precious thing in the world. We not only want to protect it; we also want it to flourish, to thrive. To a large extent, this is in our own two hands: as already discussed in chapter 5, the World Health Organization estimates that 80 percent of all heart disease, stroke, and type 2 diabetes, as well as more than 40 percent of cancer, would be prevented if Americans stopped using tobacco, ate healthy, and exercised. Taking good care of our body helps us to get the most out of our time here on Earth and increases our level of happiness—we feel better when the body feels better.

Exercise

We sit and sit. We sit at home, we sit in the car, we sit on the bus and the train, and we sit when we get to the office. We sit in class, in the library, and at the coffee shop. We sit when we eat, and when visiting or receiving friends. We sit when we are playing cards or music. We sit at the computer and in front of the television. We sit when we are sewing or doing puzzles. We sit in meditation, and while waiting at the dentist's office. Then, we sit in the dentist's chair. And in between all this sitting, we take a few steps. This is not enough movement. Some of us wear out our chairs and couches faster than we wear out our shoes.

In an earlier age we survived with what is called "persistence hunting." In persistence hunting, humans, who are slower than their prey over short distances, use a combination of running and tracking to pursue their prey until it is exhausted. We are runners by nature; two million years ago we were able to catch antelope and deer this way.

Now we have become "persistence sitters." We can "outsit" our television set and computer until they are used up and need to be replaced. We can "outsit" our car, sewing machine, and telephone until they break down. A fox that does not run does not get to eat. A pelican that does not fly does not get to catch fish. We, on the other hand, can eat without running, walking, fishing, or swimming. And we do, much to the detriment of our health.

Once again, we cannot trust our feelings about exercise. Our feelings often urge us to become couch potatoes. We need to listen to the voice of mindfulness in order to get up and exercise when we do not feel like it.

Alcohol

We each draw the line at a different place with alcohol. Buddha drew the line at zero—not surprising, considering that alcohol is an antagonist of mindfulness. Buddha was clear: alcohol causes carelessness. There is a reason why driving under the influence is against the law. Buddha made abstaining from intoxicating substances a condition for joining his community. Ever since his day, "No Alcohol" has been one of the precepts you must follow if you want to be a "card-carrying" Buddhist, even though some Zen adepts who make a virtue out of disregarding conventions joyously ignore this stricture.

It would be great if you could stand behind a line you draw with mindfulness. The problem is that mindfulness is often no longer there after the first drink, and for many people, the line becomes an indistinct blur in the sand or disappears altogether. Buddha's idea was that if you do not get started, you are safe.

Despite all the publicity from beer and wine producers, alcohol is not so harmless. It fuels arguments because it lowers inhibitions. It activates the angry fiend inside that you did not know existed. It makes you say things that you would not say when sober. Pushing each other's buttons is a favorite pastime of many couples, and alcohol makes people react strongly to provocations. This can be toxic to relationships. If your relationship is already shaky, alcohol can make it worse.

Alcohol affects your sex life negatively, as it lowers sexual sensitivity both in men and women. Especially when overused, it interferes with both men's and women's ability to enjoy sex. Those romantic images of a couple looking dreamily into each other's eyes over a glass of wine are just publicity. They are as true to life as the cigarette ads of another era, of images of the Marlboro Man riding into the sunset as an exemplar of manliness and healthy outdoor living.

Be mindful of the thought that says, "I need a drink." When it comes, take a few deep and slow breaths: time is on your side with impulses—they often fade after a few seconds. Consider that perhaps what you really need is a break of some kind. Consider these alternatives: Go for a walk in the fresh air; it will invigorate your body instead of overloading it with a basically toxic substance. Call a friend; it will gladden your heart instead of making your liver work harder. Have a cup of tea; get or give a massage; sing; have a short meditation to bring you back to yourself.

These alternatives do not produce hang-ups, headaches, or interfere with your sleep. They do not give you a beer belly, or make it illegal to drive. They do not cloud your judgment or make you pass out when you want to enjoy sexual intimacy.

What I'm suggesting is this: do not drink impulsively, mindlessly, out of habit, or because others do it. And do not drink because the ads say that it's cool.

❀

There are many volumes on healthy lifestyle choices, shelves full of them. The purpose of this short chapter is not to compete with them, but to make the important point that information is not enough for making healthy changes. If it were, many more people would stop smoking, exercise, and lose weight. Mindfulness is also necessary. That is because you must have the ability to keep your deep wish, your dream for a better life in mind all the time, in the "here and now" of the language of mindfulness teachings. It is always now, and you are always here, wherever you are. You must remember to eat better when you are shopping for food, when you are preparing food, and when you sit down to eat. You must remember to exercise when you do not feel like it, or when you feel tired. Fatigue often dissipates as you get into a badminton game, or start bicycling; and when you do not feel like it—that is the time when you need exercise most.

You will find that as your mindfulness skills get better, your ability to make healthy lifestyle changes will also improve. And with that, your feelings of happiness and well-being will grow.

Time for Practice

. . . .

Guided Meditation: You Can Choose Your Thoughts

❈

Bring your focus to the sensations coming from the body—
sensations related to breathing, to posture, and to skin.
Slow down your breathing, and be aware of tension blocks.
See how many of these you can discover in your body.
Relax them as you breathe.

❈

Try an experiment: think of a bright sunset with vivid colors,
with birds flying through the golden sky.

❈

Now, change, and think of an overcast sky with dark, menacing
clouds.

❈

Notice that feelings come along with thoughts.
While doing this exercise, you may have had good feelings,
or feelings of boredom.

❈

Remember that you brought these thoughts to mind
 intentionally.
They did not arise on their own.

❁

We have the power to change the direction of our thoughts.
We have this power all the time.
As we change our thoughts, we indirectly change our feelings.
We can mentally evoke the bright sky and good feelings follow.
We do this in our homes as a matter of course:
When the sky gets dark, we turn on the lights.
 We do not stay in darkness.

❁

Children are afraid of the dark.
 Some adults also feel uneasy in the dark.
Could it be because of the feelings it brings?

❁

What color is your sky now, the sky of your mind?
What is its brightness level?
 If there are clouds, what are they about?
We are not at the mercy of our thoughts; we can be the master.
We can assume power over our thoughts.

❁

When it gets cold and dark in the winter,
 some people head to sunnier places.
We can also do this mentally.
 We can be more positive in our thinking.
Remember: there is a sun inside each of us.
Don't let the clouds get in its way—let it shine.
Brighten up dark moments with the light of consciousness.

Practice Song: The Earth Keeps Turning

The Earth keeps turning, every mountain and sea,
The mind that keeps pace is the mind that's free.
Enjoy the changes, enjoy the day,
You're also changing as it fades away.

Feel your love, feel your peace,
Stay with the light at every turn.
Enjoy the changes, enjoy the day,
You're also changing as it fades away.

When we are in our thoughts we are not keeping up with the world. A thought is like a stick that gets in a cart wheel—it stops the wheel from turning. But the world does not wait for us. When we are lost in thought, the world keeps on going, with the result that we get out of sync with it. We are now "in our own world," not the one we share with others. This means that we are out of sync with everyone else as well.

With a free mind we are in flow. Flow is like a movie. A thought is like a snapshot.

The world that keeps turning is not only outside us—it is also inside. The inside world also keeps turning—we are getting hungry, sleepy, thirsty, tired . . . all day long, whether we are daydreaming or living in real time. We are also getting older.

It is the free mind that keeps pace with its surroundings, not the busy mind! The busy mind can be ahead of its time or behind, but it is not with it. Worse still, it is often somewhere else altogether, and not even in the picture.

In contrast, the free mind is available; it stays in touch.

Chapter 11

Connect with Compassion

Time for a Story

Seeing and Not Seeing

Ameditation student went to a well-known Zen teacher and asked him: "When you sit in meditation, do you see or not?"

The master hit him with his stick and asked: "When I hit you, does it hurt or not?" (There is a lot of "The master hit him with his stick" in Zen stories. Think of these as gentle admonishments rather than knockout blows.)

"It both does and does not hurt."

"I both see and do not see."

"How can you both see and not see?"

The master said: "What I see are the vacillations and wanderings of my own mind. What I do not see is the right and wrong and good and bad of other people. This is what I mean by seeing and not seeing."

Time for Reflection

. . . .

Just one drop of compassion is enough to bring back
spring on Earth.
—THICH NHAT HANH

What is your heart like—is it like a castle surrounded by walls? Is your heart a gated community? Or is it open like a flowering meadow? Is it inviting like a green forest? When you are open, others also open up. Each relationship is an open-ended communion. When you connect to the natural being of a person, you connect with the whole of nature through it.

Intimate and loving relationships are not only with other persons. Our relationship with nature can also be intimate and loving, and it also has an effect on our happiness level. In an urban setting, nature is suppressed. It consists mostly of other humans, dogs, the blue sky, wind and rain, the air we breathe, the water we drink, and the food we eat. Nevertheless, it is possible to develop a relationship with nature through these if we take a moment to reflect. Conscious breathing, conscious drinking, and conscious eating are opportunities to affirm our relationship to the Earth and to her creatures. Looking at the sky broadens our perspective. Looking at the sun or the stars brightens it.

I live close to a lake, and I consider myself blessed—I have access to a slice of nature. I take advantage of this opportunity to go sit by the lake when I can. I have developed a relationship with the lake. The lake is not separate from the rest of nature, and when I'm there I feel connected to all of nature. The lake mirrors the sky—it is also blue. It also mirrors the sun; each square inch of the lake reflects the sun in its own way. The waves mirror the wind.

The boats navigate their way through currents, waves, wind, at night, and in foggy weather—through uncertainty, like us.

Navigating a boat is not always smooth sailing. Like us, boats also go through stressful times during their journeys.

Connection Is a Source of Happiness

Next to the death penalty, the cruelest legal punishment humans can think of is solitary confinement—cutting off connections. The four walls cut out not just human connection, but connections to nature as well. Do not impose that on yourself. Loving, willing, empathic connection is available if you are open—if you do not close up or wait for it to come to you. The popularity of social media, emails, and text messages derives from our need for connection. However, there is more to connection than verbal connection. We also connect with our eyes, with our voices, and with other sense organs. And in some enchanted moments, we connect with our hearts.

However, at a certain level connection is always there, whether we are aware of it or not. Our feeling of separateness, that chasm we sometimes feel between our self and the rest of nature, is only an illusion created by the mind. The Earth is always pulling us close to her bosom with gravity, and the sun is always trying to enlighten us.

Urban Connections

Sharon, now happily married, used to live on the tenth floor of a condominium complex in downtown Toronto. From her balcony, all she could see were other tall buildings, roads, and parking lots. On the balcony, there was also a spindly houseplant hanging on to life in a pot that was too small for it. Sharon was concerned about its well-being, and watered it lovingly—for that plant and her boyfriend were her main connections to nature. They were her forest, vegetable garden, and extended family. Compared to the communal way we humans have lived on this planet for most of our existence, boyfriends, girlfriends, and potted plants have now assumed an overwhelming importance. Take them away, and you haven't got much left. Mostly just work, and the other potted plant lovers you meet in the elevator.

Our romantic partner has become the Most Important Person, and our relationship our anchor in the sea of life. This is a heavy burden to bear for a lover. It is a burden even for a potted plant.

❖

Beauty and the Beast

I told the story of *Beauty and the Beast* to Nadia, who was not getting along with her husband. They continued to share the same house, but in the same spirit that Palestinians and Israelis share the same land.

In that fairy tale, there is a gap that separates Beauty from the Beast. The Beast is not in Beauty's heartspace. It is with a drop of compassion that Beauty closes that gap at the end, as her feeling of separateness from him dissipates. The result is happiness for both of them.

The man is the Beast in this story, as you may have already guessed (I'm talking about the fairy tale, not the popular TV series). Before the males among us get their hackles up, though, I must tell you that in this story he is a very special kind of beast—he is actually a handsome prince. He was turned into a hideous-looking animal for a momentary lack of compassion—he refused to let a fairy in from the rain, and she turned him into a beast as punishment. Only by finding true love can the horrible curse be removed.

A subtlety is missing in the English translation: Beauty (Belle in the original French) is the given name of the heroine rather than a judgment on her looks. In French, the common name Isabelle is sometimes shortened to "Belle" as a nickname. The story specifically mentions that Belle was physically no fairer than her two sisters, but she had inner beauty. Perhaps the English title of this story should properly be *Belle and the Beast*. As it is, *Beauty and the Beast* seems to load the story with gender bias, this time slanted against the less fair sex.

Belle is kind and pure of heart, and when her father asks what to bring his daughters on his way back from a long trip, she only asks for a rose, while her two sisters ask for clothes and jewels.

Despite his repulsive looks, the Beast behaves as a kindhearted prince (which he really is) toward Belle and her father, treating them with affection and warmth. The rose that her father brings to Belle comes from the Beast's garden. But when they meet, the Beast just cannot get Belle to love him—his challenging looks prove to be too much of a barrier. Serendipitously, while she is with him, Belle keeps dreaming of a handsome prince.

One day, while she is visiting with her sisters, Belle forgets all about the Beast, and does not keep her word to return to his castle as she had promised him. However, she remembers to look at the magic mirror he had given her (a beta version of the iPhone?), and in it, she sees him dying of heartbreak under the rosebush—the same rosebush that provided her with the lovely rose. She is moved, and turns the magic ring he had also given her to instantly transport herself to his side. Her tears fall on his dying body as she says that she loves him. He is instantly revived and transformed by these words into the handsome prince of her dreams. They get married, and live happily ever after.

Folk tales sometimes tell the same story as peer-reviewed research papers, but with more charm. They are also more likely to elicit strong feelings. Here is the perennial truth: It is love, more than wealth and castles, even princely ones, that brings happiness. And even handsome princes look like beasts when at times they lack compassion. The love and the presence of a kind woman redeem a man's momentary lack of compassion in this story.

Notice that it is the man who is transformed by the relationship in this story—Belle is portrayed as a kind and beautiful spirit from the beginning, and she stays true to herself. "A rose is a rose is a rose," as Gertrude Stein once wrote in a poem. His transformation and their consequent marriage made her fulfilled, but she was a happy soul from the beginning. He, on the other hand, found happiness when he found her. Even more, he found life, as he was dying from heartbreak before.

It is easy to see this fairy tale as implying that women are all inherently bighearted. Yet, if you read it carefully, this is not in the story: Belle has two sisters who do not have the same inner beauty. They are materialistic and greedy. The story actually says that only 33 percent of women have that soul-catching inner beauty that is so engagingly extolled here.

❖

By all accounts, Nadia's husband was a challenge. But I had found through questioning her that Nadia had not said many words of appreciation to him during their twenty-five-year marriage. There was also a gap there—he was not in her heartspace. In the story, Belle had also found it difficult to say loving words to the Beast for some time.

I urged Nadia to make space for Mark in her heart, and see what happened. But twenty-five years is a long time. With the passage of time, the rivulets of compassion had already carved a path on the ground as they flowed, and they were not going near Mark anymore.

It is funny how we choose where we sprinkle our drops of compassion. Nadia chose to sprinkle many on her sick cat and her sons, but none on him.

It is true that some people are more lovable than others. Yet, those others, whose light is hidden under a bushel, need compassion as well, most likely even more.

I know how Nadia feels. I catch myself picking and choosing all the time. I also know that compassion is like oxygen—we all need some. One fortunate result of sprinkling compassion indiscriminately all around is that when we do that, some of those precious drops end up falling on us as well. This is the root of self-compassion.

When we are stingy with our compassion toward other people, we also tend to be stingy with it toward our own self. Compassion then becomes an award for those who are "good" and "deserving." We tend to hold our self to the same exacting standards as others, and suffer from oxygen deficiency as a result.

Compassion is a way of connecting. When we feel compassion, we also include. The more compassion we feel, the more inclusive our heart becomes. In the Buddhist tradition, compassion is an essential practice. "When we come in contact with the other person, our thoughts and actions should express our mind of compassion, even if that person says and does things that are not easy to accept. We practice in this way until we see that our love is not contingent upon the other person being lovable," writes Thich Nhat Hanh.

"I'm good to people who are good, but I'm also good to people who are not good—because goodness is virtue," says the *Tao Te Ching*.

Seeing compassion as a practice is a consolation—it means that just like all the other mental qualities mentioned in the Table of Contents, it can be developed through mindfulness. Without compassion, we tend to exclude people from our heart. Perhaps you have been excluded from a party once, and remember what it felt like. Those for whom we do not feel compassion are excluded from the party in our heart. "Happiness is not an individual matter," writes Thich Nhat Hanh. When the excluded is a stepchild, an older or a younger child, a brother or sister, it leaves them scarred. Eventually their unhappiness bounces back at us like a ball bouncing back from a wall. When the one who is excluded is one's life partner, the coldness they feel penetrates the walls of the house, and also chills the one who is excluding.

❖

However, beauty is not always feminine in gender.

In his *Tattoos on the Heart*, Gregory Boyle tells the story of the title of his book. While working with gang members in Los Angeles, he had been leaning hard on a particularly exasperating young man without any positive results. One day, he decided to catch this guy while he was doing the right thing, then lavish praise on him: "I tell him how heroic he is, and how the courage he now exhibits in transforming his life far surpasses the hollow 'bravery' of his barrio past. I tell him he is a giant among men." The "homie" looks at him in stunned silence for a while, and then says, "Damn G . . . I'm gonna tattoo that on my heart."

Wisdom and Compassion

The heart can also open through wisdom. Wisdom points out that I'm woven with the same elements as all other beings. We all have the same challenges and aspirations. I'm not separate from *this*; I'm not a freak of nature. Much suffering results from creating a gap between us and them, between me and her or him, between pets and farm animals, between the houseplant that I care for lovingly and the tree in the forest that I turn into lumber. That tree breathed out the oxygen that I am breathing in now. We are literally parts of the same organism. Women and men create one another. Adults and children give birth to one another. The food on my plate has the taste of the Earth.

In the end wisdom and compassion also create each other. If wisdom is not creating compassion, then it is not true wisdom—it has turned into an intellectual game separated from life.

Amazing Grace

Grace is that energy that makes the blessings of life available to all of us without regard to merit. The sun shines on all of us whether we deserve it or not. It shines equally on saints and sinners. In this respect the human world is not very "graceful." We are obsessed with fairness, justice, and merit. We make a distinction between those who are "deserving" and others. Yet, often, the undeserving need sunshine more—many criminals became involved in crime because there was not enough sunshine in their delicate lives when they were small children.

I have always admired the inspiring melody and the first line of the hymn "Amazing Grace," but I wanted new words that focused on that precious quality of grace in a positive way so that we could all experience it and identify with it. John Newton, the author of the original words, was aware of the moral shortcomings of his life—he was a slave trader by profession—and he described himself as a wretch in the second line of the hymn. I do not see myself as a wretch, and I hope that you don't either. Here we are back at chapter 2 and the pitfalls of identifying with your story. If you sing "I'm a wretch" a dozen times, you begin to believe it. This is not going to make you feel better—it is not going to make you feel happy. The author is full of admiration for the grace he sees in the world; yet, in that second line, his own gaze on himself is quite negative.

It is not enough to long for positive qualities and to admire them in the world. This is good as a first step in the right direction, but what will bring happiness to us and to others in our circle is actually embodying those qualities.

Here is my version of "Amazing Grace." I include it here because my alternate words summarize the thrust of this chapter.

> *Amazing grace, how sweet the sound,*
> *It fills the Earth and sky,*
> *Listen well and hear, look up and see,*
> *With a heart full of light and free.*
>
> *It's by grace we find our way, by grace we find love,*
> *By grace nature smiles on our day,*
> *Listen well and hear, look up and see,*
> *With a heart full of light and free.*

John Newton experienced grace firsthand: his ship was severely battered by a violent storm off the coast of Ireland; he escaped unhurt. He saw his new lease on life not as something he deserved, but something that happened through grace. My own life has also been marked by rays of grace like that; I'm sure that you can find moments of grace in your life as well.

Thich Nhat Hanh once said, "Happiness is available, please help yourself to it." To me, the message of this song is similar. Happiness is available in each moment; the blue sky is never too far—it is right above our heads—but still, some of us fail to find it. There are many currents that run through our lives. Determination and working toward one's ideal are certainly needed for achieving one's goals, but opening up to grace also helps us to enjoy life's blessings.

Seeing grace as an essential characteristic of the universe makes it easier for me to be open to it. Sing the new words to that familiar tune until you feel the energy of grace in your own heart as well.

Time for Practice

. . . .

Practice Poem: The World Is a School for Love

Love 101:
Loving your mother.
Taught by her. Course description:
see a person with her own needs,
and not only a waitress who brings you food.

Love 102:
Loving your father.
Some fail this course.
The teacher, they say,
is hard to understand.

These two are prerequisites:
fundamental courses
you need for success as a lover.
Without them, you flounder.

Love 103:
Loving your lover.
Loving someone you also need:
feeling your need as well as your love,
without letting one destroy the other.

And then,

> *Love 104:*
> *Loving your child.*
> *A being who is also a you, a fresh one,*
> *yet different*
> *and totally self-absorbed.*

> *Your child's journey begins here*
> *with your love.*
> *It is the gift that will let her*
> *love herself and thrive.*

Practice Song: Share Your Fire

> *In the fireplace of your heart*
> *Light a fire, warm up your harp,*
> *Then whoever comes along,*
> *Sing them your best love song,*
> *Give them smiles of joy,*
> *Be generous, not coy,*
> *Share your fire, share your light,*
> *In the morning and night.*

The sun shares its warmth and its light with everyone regardless of their racial background, gender, or social standing. A warm person does the same.

If you are a teacher, beware of creating "teacher's pets." Beware of excluding difficult or slower kids from a place in your heart. If you are a parent, beware of playing favorites.

The first two lines can refer to a meditation period where you specifically meditate on compassion as a quality of your heart. Sometimes compassion springs spontaneously in our hearts—maybe when we see a sick animal. That proves that compassion is there in us, but it may not be universal—we may not feel it toward all people and all animals.

The challenge is to make this occasional state of mind our default setting.

Chapter 12

Develop Your "Relationship Intelligence"

Time for a Story

The Flower Sutra

One fine summer day, the Buddha led a group of his followers on a meditative walk through the fields. He stopped by a lotus pond. Many luminous flowers were at various stages of bloom on the pond. Buddha reached out and picked one. He looked out at the members of his community who were gathering around him in a circle. He sat down. They sat down around him.

Buddha held out the flower in his hand. He did not say anything for a while, and searched the faces surrounding him. Some were expecting a talk. Others were curious. A few were confused—they were not quite sure what to make of Buddha's silent gesture. Then his gaze met Mahakashyapa's. Buddha saw a look of recognition in his eyes. They exchanged knowing smiles.

Then, Buddha spoke. He said, "The suchness of things cannot be explained by words, but must be perceived by direct experience. Mahakashyapa understands what cannot be said. I entrust him with the light of the Dharma."

Time for Reflection

. . . .

An apple is a flower that has known love.
—FÉLIX LECLERC

Are you looking for a happy relationship? Find a happy partner!
In addition, practice happiness yourself. Find the blue sky wherever you are—it is right there, above your head. It is hard to imagine two unhappy people creating a happy relationship. You do not get honey when you mix two bottles of vinegar together.

In a relationship even one unhappy partner is problematic—marriage counselors thrive on this combination. Look through the Table of Contents in this book. You need all those skills for creating happy relationships. If your partner is missing some of them, you need to be strong enough and willing to make up the deficit.

Appreciate Your Partner

Some people appreciate their partners for what they are. Others disparage them for what they are not—for what they see their partners as lacking. The butterfly zigzags through the air with staccato movements. The seagull soars smoothly. If those two got married, would they be able to enjoy each other's different way of being?

It is the attitude that determines whether the relationship is a source of nourishment or a source of stress, whether it is a source of enrichment or irritation. This is particularly true of female-male relationships: you may think that you embody human nature, that the way your body is, the way you think and feel, your hormones and metabolism are what human nature is all about. Well, it turns out that half the human race thinks otherwise. They think that your body is a little strange, your reactions to things are a little puzzling, and the way you dress, do your hair, and carry yourself are a bit peculiar. Some even think that you are so different that you might have come from a different planet . . .

Try Same-Sex Marriage . . .

The challenge of getting along with a person of the opposite sex is humorously illustrated by Garrison Keillor in his inimitable *Prairie Home Companion* radio show. In one segment, Keillor pretends to be a marriage counselor, and receives a man who complains about his wife's numerous creams and beauty products overflowing from the shelves in the bathroom: she has one cream for her eyelids and another for her earlobes, while he only has a shaver and some deodorant. He also complains about her taste in movies. Garrison asks him what he himself enjoys doing, and discovers that this man's passion is collecting old car horns, and arranging them together to play tunes. His wife does not like to listen to that. After hearing one of his car horn tunes, Garrison suggests that he should try same-sex marriage.

As in all good humor, there is a grain of truth behind that joke. Until relatively recently, women spent much of their time with other women. Our male ancestors were often away in the company of other men—in hunting parties, pirate ships, merchant marine vessels; as sailors, in army units, street gangs, trade guilds, monasteries, and as members of the Mafia. Many poignant folk songs tell the story of a young man leaving his pregnant girlfriend to go to war, or to go to sea as a sailor. In Québec, the part of Canada where I live, women were not allowed in taverns until about forty years ago. Men got together with women to have sex, but trying to coexist with women on a daily and hourly basis is a relatively recent challenge for them. Some are still reeling from the experience. The same thing is true for women also—nowadays, they initiate 75 percent of all divorces. In the United States, divorce happens, on the average, after eight years of marriage. That's how long a man and a woman are able to stand each other's close company these days. The life of the average unmarried relationship is even shorter: just two years. This may come as a surprise, but there is some research showing that on the average, gay relationships are slightly more stable, and last longer. Garrison Keillor points toward an important challenge in female-male relationships—the challenge of sharing a life with someone who is physically and emotionally so different.

This chapter on relationships comes at the end of the book, not because the subject is less important than the others, but because the mindfulness lessons in the preceding chapters all help in making a relationship better.

Apply the lessons of the previous chapters to the joy and challenge of a relationship.

Maintain a positive mood, even if your partner seems to be in a funk. That is when you need your inner sunshine the most—because now that light has to illuminate the hearts of two people.

Regulate your moods so that irritation or anger do not stay long and poison your day. Now, your day is shared. Any toxicity you introduce into it also affects your partner.

Indeed, each chapter has something to contribute to improving and maintaining a relationship.

Yin and Yang

Sexism would make no sense in the context of Taoism, as in that tradition the universe is seen as made up of the interplay between the forces of Yin (the receptive or female) and Yang (the active or male). An attitude that emphasized one at the expense of the other would naturally be lopsided. As a longtime T'ai Chi practitioner, I am reminded of the necessity for the balance between these two forces during every T'ai Chi session. Most people start T'ai Chi practice with plenty of active energy, but with a deficit of receptive energy. This is true of women as well as men. Beware of this dynamic in relationships.

A push is an example of active energy. In T'ai Chi play, instead of resisting or pushing back, we get our center out of the way so that the push does not unbalance us. The other person's energy encounters no resistance. She was expecting some resistance, so she probably put some weight behind her push and leaned into it. Now that weight continues to pull her forward into empty space. A good T'ai Chi practitioner just "helps" her sparring partner go where apparently she wanted to go with that push—she gently pulls her into the void toward which she is leaning. The result can be surprising. An unwary pusher can go tumbling across the room with only a minimum of help from her sparring partner. In T'ai Chi, we use the other person's energy to win during skirmishes.

In a relationship, pushing back is not the only way to deal with an aggressive partner. Do not underestimate the power of equanimity. Get your center out of the way so that the pushing does not unbalance you—do not take things personally. In a discussion, do not counter force with force. Be receptive and try to understand the other person's needs and emotions. Faced with such receptive energy, force will soon spend itself.

"Yin is the mother of Yang," say the Taoists. Try this little experiment: extend your arm as if you are pushing something. Feel your muscles working. Notice that your ability to push is good for a foot or two. Once your arm is fully extended, your ability to push is spent. Now Yang turns to Yin. Such a moment is a good time to respond in T'ai Chi play.

Sexual Attraction

Attraction of one kind or another is literally what keeps everything going in the universe: it keeps the electrons circling the nucleus of an atom; it keeps the planets circling around the sun. Without attraction, the world would come apart. "I'm here for the Samsara," said a T-shirt I recently saw on a young woman. T-shirt wisdom is a mixed bag, but that one drew my attention. I felt like saying, "Me, too!" *Samsara* is relieved by occasional glimpses of Nirvana for me.

That makes it all the more poignant, and helps keep me sane at the same time. *Samsara* is the repeating cycle of birth, life, and death. It is fueled in part by sexual attraction. Often the bait of that attraction is beauty, the kind of beauty that is in the eye of the beholder. The taste of *samsara* is different from the taste of its opposite, Nirvana—as different as life in the world from life in a monastery. Nirvana is more like an alien looking at our obsessions—violence, sexual play, and the rest—from outer space, and contemplating it with a mix of curiosity and amusement.

Relationship Intelligence

There was a time when people thought that there was only one kind of intelligence. IQ reigned supreme as the measure of that all-encompassing mental capacity. Then, two psychologists, John Mayer and Peter Salovey, coined the term "emotional intelligence" to refer to a kind of smartness that IQ scores did not measure. Daniel Goleman popularized the term, and showed that it was an important measure of success in many areas.

I would like to suggest that "relationship intelligence" is a distinguishable kind of intelligence that is a measure of relationship success. We all know, or have heard of, people who are successful in many areas—such as in school, in friendships, and in their careers—but whose relationships are disasters. These people may not be particularly deficient in emotional intelligence. Relationship intelligence refers specifically to a deep understanding of what makes another person tick, and further, to an acceptance of those characteristics. In relationships, understanding another is not enough if that understanding is coupled with rejection or disdain. It must go hand in hand with sympathy, empathy, appreciation, cherishing, and even some measure of admiration. These mental states make love possible.

Different preferences, priorities, and ways of doing things wait to ambush a couple at every turn. Without relationship intelligence, this could lead to arguments, a breakup, or even a visit to the emergency ward.

Don't Let the Mind Get in the Way

In a relationship we are on the same side; we are not in competition. Yet, if one partner acts or speaks in an abrasive way, this can influence the tone of a conversation. It can get the other partner's "hackles up." Literally, hackles are the feathers on a bird's neck, or the hairs on a dog's neck. They stand up when the animal is angry or aggressive. Although we humans do not have neck feathers, we, also, may experience tension in the neck when we have an angry or threatened attitude. Be aware of tension in the neck! When our hackles are up, a discussion leans more toward an argument than toward a voyage of mutual discovery. Each partner is defending a territory instead of engaging in a mutual, wide-eyed journey of exploration.

Certainty—A Red Flag

Many species of animals have long-term relationships with their mates. They are lucky because they do not get into arguments with their mates the way we do. The other morning, I innocently remarked to my partner, Suzanne, that it was a very long freight train that I was hearing. We live about a mile from the tracks, and I had heard a familiar rumble. She listened, and declared that it was not a train, but a distant plane. We were each firm in our convictions, but soon the conversation turned to other things because we did not have any emotional investment in the matter. Imagine what may have happened if we were discussing something that was important in our lives!

Perceptions, specifically erroneous perceptions, are an important topic in Buddhism. A perception adds the element of interpretation to what may originally have been a simple sensation. "I sometimes *feel* that I am right. I do not *know* that I am," said Albert Einstein. The feeling of certainty is just that, a feeling. It is not knowledge. But not all of us have Einstein's discriminating mind, and we confuse feeling with knowledge.

Certainty plays a part in shipwrecked relationships. "You are not doing your share of the housework," is a common complaint tinged with certainty. Yet when marriage counselors ask each partner what percent of the housework they do, they often find that each partner thinks that they do about 75 percent.

Do not be gripped by the feeling of certainty. Instead, see it as an alert, and keep an open mind.

Come Out of Your Bubble

A relationship is a good way to come out of your bubble. But first, become aware of your bubble!

I was in a bubble as a teenager, but I did not know it.

Next step: start connecting to whatever is outside your bubble. Fall in love.

When we first fall in love, we tend to fall in love with an idealized version of a person. That tends to create tension between the flesh-and-blood person in front of us and the stubborn idealization we have of her. The tension is between moving out of the bubble and staying in it. The idealized version is our own creation. The person in front of us is her own person. A sustained relationship can slowly destroy the idealized image and the love that went with it. Still, you have to start somewhere.

Third step: relationships.

In the second step, confronting the reality of the loved one may destroy love. In the third step, it makes love grow. There is acceptance.

Work in progress: conscious relationships.

Can the peace and calm you developed through your mindfulness practice stand the test of everyday life with someone who is both like you and also inevitably somewhat different? Are you willing to examine your habitual patterns of thought and grow beyond them? Will you embrace this joyful exit from the bubble?

The Nature of Mind

As mapped out by neuroscientists, the brain has more regions than Canada has provinces, and just like in Canada, each region sometimes has a different opinion about things. During a relationship problem, for example, the amygdala, the seat of raw emotions, can be saying one thing; the hippocampus, the seat of memory, another; and the prefrontal cortex, the rational brain, might just be going, "tsk, tsk." There is much wisdom in the mindfulness teachings that urge us to take the voice of the brain with a grain of salt.

In a discussion, my brain sometimes pushes me to try to dominate, but not always. The person I'm discussing with makes a difference. In the presence of someone who is pushing me, something also awakens in me, and wants to compete and to try to push back. But if I'm with someone who is simply musing, who is not pushing, my mind is awakened in a different way. I'm inspired—I'm discovering myself. My competitive instincts are temporarily asleep; they are staying out of the way.

With mindfulness it is possible to guide a conversation so that it resembles a poem rather than a brief in a court of law. Awareness of sensations, feelings, and perceptions is not only something to be practiced on the meditation cushion. This awareness also helps us to avoid collisions during a conversation.

❖

"The purpose of human life is to be happy," said the Dalai Lama. As I look around, I see this purpose more consistently expressed in the lives of women. Many men slip into following their evolutionary roles of striving, competing, and dominating. Perhaps this is their idea of happiness, but the collateral damage from this "happiness" is enormous: in 2014, there were eighteen ongoing wars or serious armed conflicts in the world, and about twenty million refugees. Ninety percent of all casualties were civilians, including women and children. In 2015, the refugee count reached an unprecedented sixty million.

Mindfulness practice can help men become aware of their biases. Buddha is a good example for us: by birth, he was born into the Kshatriya (warrior) caste. After a six-year period of meditation and retreat, he renounced his fighter heritage against all the expectations of his father. He embraced many gender-neutral values, and tirelessly promoted peace and compassion for the rest of his life.

Time for Practice

Meditation Theme: Visit an "Inner Beauty Salon"

Being in the moment makes one ageless! We do not have to carry all those years that are behind us on our backs, like a load of bricks. They have all fluttered away like butterflies, and with mindfulness, the same freshness of experience that delights a child is available to all of us, regardless of age.

Beauty salons specialize in external beauty—beauty of hair, skin, eyes, and nails. Inner beauty has more to do with letting shine the beauty of nature we already possess as women and men. Trees, flowers, and birds need no makeup to look good. Are humans the only exception?

Many classical sculptors and painters have expressed inner beauty while portraying outer beauty.

What makes a human being beautiful?

What would happen in an "inner beauty salon"?

"What do I need to do in order to be more beautiful?"

Use this question as a meditation theme, like a Zen koan, and sit with it.

Practice Song: Love the Apple Tree

Often our needs, our wants, and our love are quite mixed up. This song is designed to throw some light on this mixture, and hopefully also increase the proportion of love in it.

Love the apple tree, not just the taste of its fruit,
Love the rosebush, not just the smell of its flower,
Love the honeybee, not just the honey in the jar,
Love the garden, love the garden,
In the spring, and in the winter.

Love the sparrow, not just its voice and its song,
Love the river, not just its water in the shower,
Love the artist, not just the colors of her flowers,
Love the Earth, love the Earth
In the spring, and in the winter.

This song is ostensibly about our attitude toward the Earth, and how we "love" bits and pieces of nature, but only in relation to our needs. However, it applies equally well to relationships. There also, the challenge is to love the whole person, and not only parts of her personality or body, her taste in cars, or her way with food.

Afterword

I started this book by mentioning that some people seem to be born with a sunny temperament—they seem to be happy by nature. When I was younger, I had a wistful fascination with such people and their effortless good humor. I did not consider myself one of them. I found happiness by observing my happier friends and their families, and by following the practice and the example of my teacher, Thich Nhat Hanh.

As the book progressed, I had the occasion to reconnect with a few of these "naturally happy" people I had known earlier. I noticed to my surprise that the happiness and good nature I had seen decades ago were no longer there in all of them, or they were reduced. "The slings and arrows of outrageous fortune," as Shakespeare put it, had taken their toll, as had career reversals. And more important, those inevitable dark clouds that are woven into every life—sickness, old age, loss, and death.

The "happiness gene," if it exists, seems to be more evident in the carefree days of youth than in maturity and old age.

"Happiness Gene" vs. Happiness Skills

Indeed, happiness skills may be more effective than that elusive happiness gene for lifelong well-being. A sunny disposition does not necessarily make you take good care of yourself. It does not induce you to exercise, eat well, or not smoke. These precautions might not

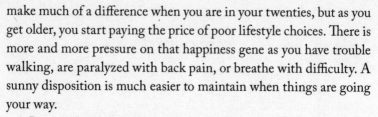

make much of a difference when you are in your twenties, but as you get older, you start paying the price of poor lifestyle choices. There is more and more pressure on that happiness gene as you have trouble walking, are paralyzed with back pain, or breathe with difficulty. A sunny disposition is much easier to maintain when things are going your way.

Loss, sickness, old age, and death are part of life—there is no life without them. They are part of a happy, as well as an unhappy, life. Yet, those issues are not the primary focus of positive psychology. They are not the favorite topic of pop psychology, either. However, Buddha was concerned with them from the beginning of his quest. His hand of wisdom can guide us through our entire journey, and not abandon us when we need it most. Buddha's teachings are specifically designed to promote acceptance, to bring our focus to the present moment, and to help us enjoy the life we touch with our senses. The happiness they bring can accompany us through life. Glance through the Table of Contents to review its essentials. In this book they are presented as applied to my own life, and to the lives of people with whom I am familiar.

The Challenge of the Media

I set out to write a book about happiness. I had to work at keeping my focus there instead of on unhappiness—for wherever I look, I see unhappiness discussed, analyzed, and even glorified. Not only in books, but also in movies, songs, and on TV. Yes, psychology has redeemed itself, and turned its face toward happiness with the result that there is now a substantial body of psychological literature on positive psychology. But what we consume as readers, moviegoers, and television watchers is more than books about psychology. So far as I can tell, there has not been a corresponding movement toward positive literature—positive moviemaking, fiction, and songwriting. When my partner and I watch a movie, we do not want to spend our time watching unhappy people make a mess of things—this is not our idea of entertainment. Yet, when we look at what is playing in the movie theaters, we find a lot of that. We have to search in order to find positive, inspiring movies. I run against the same thing when I'm looking for new songs to enjoy. Instead of inspiration, I find much complaining, bitching, and unhappiness set to music. Music fills the mind, but this is not what I want to fill my mind with. Mindfulness of what we take in, of what we watch, read, and listen to, is important in setting our compass toward a positive view of life.

We also need positive religion and positive spirituality—as much as we need positive psychology. We need to replace some of the talk about going to heaven when we die with a focus on happiness here and now. Let us focus on this life rather than an afterlife. Let us focus on a here-and-now Karma, the happiness altruistic actions bring here and now rather than their possible result in the future, and let's do the right thing for the sheer joy of it rather than for the promise of a payoff.

Happiness Is Wisdom

Our wisdom is in our attitude and our lifestyle—it is not separate from those, and it is reflected in our level of happiness.

I learned much about the relevance of mindfulness for my own happiness from Thich Nhat Hanh through the twenty-five years I have known him. In this book I have shared what I learned, and also pointed to specific ways of applying mindfulness to our lives that I discovered myself. It is my sincere hope this book will be of benefit to its readers.

Acknowledgments

First, I acknowledge my debt to Thich Nhat Hanh with gratitude. Without him and his teachings this book would not have been written. Many of the songs and practices in it have been inspired by him—by a sentence casually uttered during a talk at Plum Village, a line of his poetry, or an answer he gave to a question.

I appreciate his confidence in appointing me a Dharma teacher in his lineage, and I appreciate the warmth of his community, as they adopted many of my practice songs. Thich Nhat Hanh's books can be read as companion volumes for going more deeply into some of the topics I discuss here.

Many thanks to İlkay Bilgişin. He is the best friend that I mentioned in chapter 1, the bright light of my teenage years, and my college roommate. He is one of my two happiness models. My other happiness model has been my partner, Suzanne Forest. These people naturally possess many of the qualities I describe in this book. I consider myself fortunate to have known them well.

I would also like to thank Paul Century and Kirsten Anderson for adding their musical gifts to the songs, Paul with his guitar and Kirsten with her voice. You can listen to their contributions at MindfulnessMeditationCentre.org/finding-the-blue-sky/.

Valerie Legge and Chantal Jacques read the manuscript and shed light on some of my blind spots with their suggestions. Thanks also to Andrew Yackira, my editor at TarcherPerigee, for helping to tweak the title of this book, and for his enthusiastic encouragement along the way.